Helping Teens in Crisis

Helping Teens In *CRISIS*

Miriam Neff

Tyndale House Publishers, Inc.
Wheaton, Illinois

Library of Congress Cataloging-in-Publication Data

Neff, Miriam.
      Helping teens in crisis / Miriam Neff.
          p.   cm.
      ISBN 0-8423-6823-X
      1. Teenagers—Counseling of.   2. Adolescent psychology.
  I. Title.
      HV1431.N44   1993
      362.7'083—dc20   92-42900

Printed in the United States of America

99 98 97 96 95 94
9   8   7   6   5   4   3

Dedication

*To the teens at my school who have opened
their lives and hearts to me during their
moments of crisis. I have seen courage and
grit, ordinary living and miracles; and
sometimes the ordinary living is more the
miracle, considering the mountains they must
face.*

*And to my four children, who were all teens
at once, translating my profession into a
twenty-four-hour learning binge, forcing me
to be a quick study with my heart on my
sleeve and frequently my foot in my mouth:
Valerie, 21 and no longer my child but forever
my daughter, my friend; John, my gentle
puzzle who taught me parenting with an open
hand; Charles, through whom we are
learning the power of No; and Robb, whom I
quote: "You don't need a reason to be happy."*

*And to all parents: I humbly salute you.
There is no greater, more challenging job.*

﹍Contents﹍

⟵Foreword⟶

Crises take many forms. And the severity of our crises vary through the years. When I was a young child, my most severe crisis might have been breaking an arm or losing a pet. During adolescence, crises for my peers and me might have involved disintegrating relationships or less-than-acceptable grades.

Today, however, I find that the teenage crises are much more serious, involving problems such as pregnancy, alcohol, drugs, and running away. It's not that those situations didn't exist during my youth, but these days they seem almost epidemic and have become the primary crises. Today's teenagers live in a difficult, even dangerous world.

Young people seldom experience a crisis in isolation; people who care for them are also affected. Parents, for example, become aware of their kids' crises through a variety of signals. It may be a shrill telephone ring in the dead of night, falling grades and decreased motivation, dramatic changes in appearance or behavior, glazed eyes and reeking breath . . . or an official visit by the police.

Whatever the cause or symptoms, crises can lead to pain, confusion, frustration, estrangement, and bitterness.

Hurting kids need help, and caring parents need answers and support.

Miriam Neff understands the crises faced by teens and their parents. As a high-school counselor, she has met with hundreds of young people, moms, and dads face to face. She has heard their stories, felt their pain, and offered help. Miriam also knows the crises firsthand, as a parent, having dealt with problems in her own family. She has written this book, *Helping Teens in Crisis*, to offer her expertise and counsel to hurting parents and kids.

With empathetic understanding, Miriam guides us through the world of teenagers—a world filled with life-altering decisions—a world very different from what adults remember from their own adolescent years. And as one committed to Jesus Christ, Miriam writes from a strong Christian perspective. She gives insight; she gives answers; she gives hope.

This book is a must for any caring adult who knows or lives with a teenager in crisis.

JOSH MCDOWELL

▂ 1 ▂
A Day in the Life
of Carrie

6:45 A.M. Friday morning. Carrie hoped she could get out of the house without talking to her mom. She shook her still-damp hair and threw the hair-spray bottle into her bulging bag. An ordinary day—almost. No time for food. She shouldered her bag, pushed in an extra pair of gym shoes and a jacket. She turned sideways down the hall so the swaying bag would not bang the walls. Waking up Dad, if he was in town, was not smart.

She stopped at the refrigerator. She stuffed a diet soda into her gym shoe, placing it carefully so it would not touch her algebra assignment. Mr. Thomas would not accept wrinkled papers. She opened another soda for the road.

"Carrie, I didn't see you last night."

Oops! She'd missed her escape!

"I didn't want to wake you up. I thought you were tired. Chris helped me with my algebra. I was home by eleven, I think."

"Do you have plans this weekend? I was hoping we could do something together. Maybe go to Springhill Mall?" Carrie's mother pushed her slightly graying hair back and poured herself a cup of black coffee. She eyed her daughter with affection twinged with concern and curiosity. "We haven't even been to McDonald's for months."

"Mom, tonight's prom! Remember?" Carrie knew she sounded exasperated. "I'll miss my bus." She needed aspirin. For once the bottle was in the drawer by the door. The aspirin bottle settled in, dislodging the soda can from her gym shoe.

"We'll talk later," her mom called. Carrie was halfway down the walk.

"Nancy, you still here?" The muffled voice from the back bedroom sounded reasonable.

Nancy put down the now-empty coffee cup. "Yes, but I've got to leave for work. Will you make sure Matthew catches his bus?" Nancy knew that Matthew could manage on his own. Her thirteen-year-old son was pretty responsible, she thought with pride. Walking to her car, she could see Carrie's bus down the street. There was no mistaking Carrie. Biggest book bag. Her car and Carrie's bus headed in opposite directions.

Help for knowing your teen—Chapter 3
Help for communicating—Chapter 4

Carrie hesitated at the cafeteria door. The deafening noise of hundreds of teenagers erected an invisible barrier, effectively excluding all faculty members but those assigned cafeteria duty. Carrie searched for his face. He was laughing. Jumbled feelings—too warm—happy—a little afraid. How could Jeff act regular on a day like today?

A more than gentle shove propelled her into the masses. "YOU'RE MISSING THE PLANNING!" Nichele practically yelled in her ear. "WE'RE GOING TO GET DRESSED AT MISSY'S HOUSE. CAN I BORROW YOUR HAIR SPRAY?"

Carrie squeezed near the cafeteria table to rest her bag and relieve her shoulder.

"DON'T FORGET TO BRING THOSE SHOES!"

Why does Nichele always practically yell? Carrie thought, feeling irritated.

"Ryan's brother made the reservations," Chris announced.

"You mean for dinner?" Carrie glanced across the cafeteria again at Jeff. Didn't he even know she was here?

"No, silly. The Radisson. We have a suite. Everybody owes him ten dollars. I'm collecting."

"I don't think we're going," Carrie whispered to Nichele.

"JEFF TOLD RYAN YOU ARE!"

Announce it to the world, Carrie thought. Mom better not hear about this! The first bell blared above the din. Bodies rose in unison from the benches. Waves of jeans and T-shirts moved toward the hallways. Carrie tried to edge toward the trash barrel with her empty soda can. Her stomach rumbled. *I hope it doesn't do that in Algebra,* she thought.

She threw the can.

A hand intercepted it in front of the barrel.

"Missed!" It was him. Carrie grinned. "You're bringing your suit tonight, aren't ya? Some of us wanna swim."

"Uhh, sure."

"Dan and I can pick you up at Missy's. What time?"

"Dan? I thought we were going with Nichele and Sam."

Jeff turned toward Hall D, giving her book bag a

parting tug. "Nichele would drown out the music. She's so loud she drives me crazy. We're going with my friends. You'll see her at the party anyway. See ya later."

Help for understanding male/female differences—Chapter 5

Nancy stopped in the coffee room. She filled her mug half full and then opted for a generous dose of cream to fill her cup. Funny how black coffee tasted better a few years ago. Her supervisor joined her.

"How's the family?"

"Fine. Doing fine."

"I think we're going to get the Radisson award this month. You did a nice piece of work setting up that report. It's not just based on our high occupancy; the customer satisfaction ratings were our highest."

Nancy smiled. At least some things in her life really were "fine."

He watched Matthew walk slowly across the neighbor's yard. *The kid was too quiet,* Arnie thought. The phone rang. Why was there *always* only a third of a cup of coffee left in the pot? He cradled the phone between shoulder and ear while searching the fridge for juice. Yes, he could get to Dayton for a one o'clock meeting. He knew the United Express schedule by heart. He'd be too tired to come back tonight. He asked to be booked to return on a morning flight—not too early. Didn't he have enough seniority to *not* be the salesman called in at the last minute? on Friday no less?

Help for changing families—Chapter 4
Help in understanding teens' new world—Chapter 2

Carrie ducked into the washroom. Dropping her bag with a thud, she looked in the mirror and groaned. *Yuk!* she thought. Flat bangs. Running her fingers through her permed hair, she lifted and sprayed, lifted and sprayed. She glimpsed a familiar face. *Gotta get outta here,* she thought. Seeing Jeff's old girlfriend made her feel uncomfortable. She looked too pretty. Well, maybe *pretty* was not the word. Grown-up. Ann had "the look." Guys stared, or at least looked two or three times. Disgustingly skinny. There had been rumors about her. Missy heard that Ann had had an abortion. Nichele said that was ridiculous—and she said it loudly. Carrie refused to think about that.

Now she really had to rush. She swung her book bag in front of her. It made an effective shield as she darted in and out, down the crowded hallway.

"Pass your homework forward." Mr. Thomas was okay.

He didn't make you feel stupid when you asked a question. Carrie reached for her homework. Something felt damp. Trouble. She extracted her folder from the bag. *How could I have left my folder open?* She peeled the algebra paper from the sweating pop can. *Out of luck. No way,* reason told her. The room had emptied. Mr. Thomas was looking at her. "I'll accept your homework if it's in my mailbox by sixth period."

Relief. She'd recopy it the first thing before she went in the lunch room. "Thanks." She was out the door to History. Algebra was the one class that mattered to her. She hadn't admitted that to anyone but her counselor.

History was different. Mr. Machine taught the class. Actually his name was Dr. Kriegbaum—but he was Mr. Machine the moment the bell rang. Actually he didn't teach the class: he turned on the overhead, his mouth moved, he wrote, he pointed. The class, the students, that is, were nonexistent. Carrie's body stayed in the room, but her mind left.

She needed a ride to Missy's by five. Her mom might be home. But maybe not. No. She'd better be out before her mom got home. That way she wouldn't have to make up answers. She'd leave a note that she was dressing at Missy's and . . . and that she was sleeping over at Chris's after the prom. That was kinda true. Some kids were having breakfast there. Chris's parents were out of town.

"I'm sure you included information about the effects of the great famine on your population study of Europe. It was thoroughly covered in Lecture 29. Leave those reports in the bin by the door. Have a good weekend." Carrie's mind returned abruptly.

She whispered hoarsely to Joe, "Did he tell us those were due today?"

"Of course not. It was on printout number 3,567." Carrie couldn't quite smile at the joke. "You might as well type out of the phone book for his reports. He wouldn't notice. I don't think he reads them. What's up, Carrie? Distracted by going out with the big guy?"

"He's not a big guy."

"He talks big."

They made their way toward the gym. It was nice to have a friend like Joe. *This must be how it feels to have a brother you like,* Carrie thought. Her little brother Matthew was okay. He was just different. With Joe it didn't matter if your bangs were flat. They'd been in swim club together as freshmen. Joe was always asking her to come to some group. Maybe she would. It would be nice to spend more time with Joe. She had to drop out of the club because she couldn't get rides home from practice. Maybe when she got her license? Then she wouldn't need rides. Then she and Joe could share that comfortable old friendship.

"I didn't know you and Jeff were going out." Joe gave another swimmer a high five passing in the crowded hallway.

"We're not. Well . . . we went to the mall and hung out at a couple of parties and talked. A lotta my friends are his friends. Going to the prom, well, it's just kind of a group thing."

They stopped in front of the girls' locker room. "Do you know him very well?" Joe always seemed really interested in her. She knew she could give him an honest answer.

"Not really. My friends think I'm lucky. He's a senior. He could have asked anybody . . . probably."

The bell rang. Joe leaned down to her ear. "You're a . . ." He started over awkwardly. "He . . ."

"I gotta go, Joe."

"Don't give him anything to brag about." Joe squeezed her arm and loped off to the boys' locker room.

Carrie pulled on her moist gym shoes and decided she'd think about what Joe meant later. She also decided not to put cold soda cans in her book bag. But she had decided that before. And then she decided she'd volunteer to be soccer goalie. She just didn't have the energy to run this morning.

Help for teens to feel good about themselves—Chapter 6

12:35 P.M. Carrie placed the neat paper in Mr. Thomas's mailbox. Relieved, she raced to her locker, grabbed her soda, and headed for the cafeteria. Fridays were always the noisiest, but today felt electric. Her head was throbbing. She went through the hot line for pizza and headed for her group. A unified "YEAH" went up from the group and was almost drowned by applause.

"I must have missed something good," Carrie said to no one in particular.

"YOU MISSED THE VOTE!" Nichele had no difficulty being heard above the noise.

"What vote?"

"Don't tell," Jeff answered. "I'll tell her later."

"Nichele, could your mom pick me up on the way to Missy's?"

"NO PROBLEM. EXCEPT IT'LL COST YA CAUSE YOU AND JEFF DUMPED SAM AND ME TO GO WITH DAN."

"Sorry. We'll see you there. Jeff didn't say anything to me about going with Dan and Rita. I'll feel stupid. I mean

. . . I don't know either of them. I wish we were going with you. Remember, you promised we'd stick together there. Watch for me, okay?"

The intercom crackled: "ALL UPPERCLASSMEN RE-PORT TO THE AUDITORIUM SEVENTH PERIOD FOR THE ASSEMBLY. REPEAT—SEVENTH PERIOD CANCELED FOR UPPERCLASSMEN. REPORT TO THE AUDITORIUM AND SIT WITH YOUR HOMEROOM."

"Thank God! I didn't have my English outline cards done for today anyway," Chris exclaimed with relief. Carrie was not spared English. She had it eighth period.

2:40 P.M. "I will now collect your outline cards." Ms. G's voice was soothing. She reviewed the time schedule for writing their papers. "We'll work in the writing lab on Mondays and Tuesdays. Make sure you bring your own disc formatted ahead of time."

Carrie tried hard to concentrate. But the assembly movie crowded out Ms. G's face. She kept seeing the accident scene. The car crushing like an accordion, the red blood oozing from the bottom of the car door. Why do they show that gore on prom day anyway? How to wreck your mood!

And mixing drinking and driving . . . now, someone should show her dad that movie. Probably adults like her dad produced the movie!

Help when teens are exposed to alcohol/drugs—Chapter 10

"Carrie. Carrie." Ms. G's voice registered finally. Carrie had no clue whether she was being asked a question or what.

"C-can I have a pass?" Carrie managed to ask. "I'll be back in five minutes. I'm sorry."

Ms. G met her by the door. "Are you feeling okay?"

"I just have a headache." Carrie walked slowly to her locker and fished for the aspirin bottle. She walked to the nearest drinking fountain. Bending over she stared closely at a large wad of purple gum stuck on the fountain. *Don't get too close,* she thought. *AIDS.*

She tossed her head back to swallow the aspirin. Looking up for some strange reason, she asked the ceiling a question. "Why do kids die young? Like in the assembly movie? Young. Free. Just partying." She knew her five minutes were up. She would put that out of her mind, too.

Back in the English room the soothing tones of Ms. G took over. "You've picked most interesting topics. Quite relevant not just to yourselves but to many people. Global Warming, New Race and Face in Eastern Europe, The ex-KGB—Its Future, Preserving the Forests. Carrie, will you tell the class your topic?"

"Air Pollution—The Year 2000."

"Good! We'll have some interesting discussions." The assembly movie did a freeze frame in Carrie's mind. She saw the red ooze from the car door and drip on the pavement.

Saved by the bell. She would not have to describe her outline. Somehow pollution seemed unimportant at the moment.

3:30 P.M. Nancy looked from her computer screen out the office window. Tired eyes. She stood up, straightening her back. Mentally she calculated that she could not finish this spreadsheet by six o'clock. Should she call home? A cold soda would give her a quick pick-up.

"Will you be able to finish that tonight?" Her supervisor seemed anxious. "There's one small change from those original figures."

"No problem." Mentally she postponed her home phone call to five o'clock. Carrie's prom night. She'd call and wish her a wonderful evening. Matthew could take a few pictures of his sister. On second thought, Nancy decided that the picture idea was not so good. Simple cooperation seemed beyond her children these days.

Maybe she'd call Arnie's office. Now that was an improbable solution. Why did the thought even cross her mind?

"Here are those corrections. And a soda. Diet 7-Up, right?"

At least I'm appreciated here, Nancy thought.

5:00 P.M. Arnie glanced at his watch. *This deal is going down the drain,* he thought, *and I couldn't care less.* Outwardly he smiled as if he were listening. He tried to remember if there was a sports bar near his hotel. No matter. He could pick up some lime juice and Vodka to take to his room. He just felt like being alone tonight.

The phone rang, and rang, and rang. Finally a drowsy Matthew answered. "I guess I just went to sleep, Mom. No. Not long ago. Yeah, it was Nichele's car. How can Carrie stand that girl? She's so LOUD. She said she told you that stuff. Mom, how should I know? Mom, you shoulda seen the *junk.* Yeah, her book bag. Yeah, that stupid dress. And her suitcase.

"The chalkboard? Okay. It says, 'Dayton—be home Saturday—Always Arnie.' Good ole "Always Arnie," huh Ma? Can Jason sleep over? Can we order a pizza? Yeah. Yeah. Thanks Ma."

Help for families who don't fit together—Chapter 3

The windows steamed from body heat. *This is no party. I can't breathe. I didn't know all these people were invited.* The suite was packed. Carrie was pushed closer to the wall as the door opened and four more people piled in. Jeff seemed to have disappeared—to Carrie's relief. He was starting to act strange.

"LET'S FIND THE BATHROOM OR BEDROOM OR ANY-WHERE ELSE. THERE'S GOTTA BE MORE SPACE HERE SOMEWHERE." Nichele pulled on Sam's arm and Carrie followed.

The prom dinner had been okay—if you like chicken. And the dance—it started out great. Who wouldn't want to be dancing with Jeff? But he kept leaving with Dan. By the last song, Carrie was ready to leave. Driving here—that was another story.

The bedroom door opened. Jeff gestured grandly for them to enter. "My girl!" He grabbed Carrie too roughly; his old girlfriend, Ann, seemed glued to his back. His jacket and tie were gone and his shirt was unbuttoned to his cummerbund. Could this be the same Jeff that was in the cafeteria this morning? The smell. The crowd. Jeff's watery eyes. It was all wrong.

"We were just going for a swim, girl." The raised buttons on his shirt gouged her bare shoulder and cheek. He leaned into her hard. "Wo-o-o-ah!" They would have toppled forward together but someone was in the door-way.

"THERE'S NO ROOM TO FALL DOWN, SAM. WE'RE OUTTA HERE!" Nichele and Sam headed back into the suite's living room. Carrie wished she was making an exit, too.

"C'mon my little swimmer. Dan and I will . . . Dan and I . . . trunk . . . YES." Jeff was now leaning back for support.

Dan finished his sentence. "We'll bring your things to the pool. Your stuff's in my trunk, isn't it?"

"Yeah. Who else is going swimming?"

"Ev—everybudy," Jeff slurred.

2:00 A.M. Perspiration ran from Carrie's temples. "I gotta jump in the pool." She stepped out of the hot tub. Maybe she could get away from Jeff.

"I'm with ya." Jeff was on her heels.

She took three quick steps and started to dive. Some weight held her back. Jeff was trying to dive in with her. She heard her shins meet cement. Water. Air. A heavy weight. Bubbles. The sound of gurgling. *Kick, Carrie!* an inner voice pleaded. One leg moved. The other was immobilized with excruciating pain! *Kick the weight away!* the inner voice pleaded. Her foot pushed against Jeff. He was between her and air.

She gulped. She thought her lungs would explode. Pressure. Panic. She kicked and flailed. Were minutes or hours passing? In slow motion the body above her rolled down, gurgling noisily. A sense of exhilarating relief swept through her as she sensed her body rising. The weight holding her down was gone.

Surface! Air! The room moved in a blur. Tread. Pain! She went under again. *Tread water, Carrie,* the inner voice insisted. The room reappeared. A security guard was leaning over the hot tub. Carrie grabbed the edge and pulled herself out. Another mind seemed to take over. The noise level was rising around the guard. Carrie hobbled into the dressing area nearby. She remembered the phone from when she had visited this Radisson with her mom. She pushed the operator digit. Ahh, the familiar tone. She dialed home.

"Mom? Mom? Yeah. No, I'm fine—I mean okay. Just . . . just . . . come pick me up? Please?"

2:30 A.M. A car pulled into a black parking lot. A mom braked abruptly beside a young girl shivering under a damp towel. The harsh bronze glare of the hotel side entrance pushed back the blackness as mother and daughter hugged. The girl's stomach rejected its contents. Mom bent over her, wrapping her jacket over her wet, tangled hair. The wail of an ambulance was unheard by either.

"Take me home, Mom." A sense that Jeff was not all right sent another shiver through Carrie. "I just wanna be safe."

As their car exited the parking lot, an ambulance and two squad cars braked at the side entrance.

— 2 —
What the World Is Like for Teens

Today's teens live in a dangerous world. A day in the life of Carrie is based on a real person. She and Jeff made different choices. Carrie is alive; Jeff drowned on prom night. My peers in the faculty cafeteria debate about which generation had the hardest teen years. But we don't argue over which lived with more *dangerous* choices. Statistics tell us some frightening facts about our teens' world and the choices they are making.

- 1 out of 4 high schoolers drink more than once a week
- 4 out of 10 teenage girls experience pregnancy
- 1 in 4 have considered suicide

- 1 in 7 have attempted suicide
- 2 leading causes of death for teens are automobile accidents involving alcohol, and suicide
- 7 out of 10 have tried marijuana

I can't resolve the debate over which generation had the greatest struggle during the teen years. I doubt if our faculty will, or any parent group, church board, or government committee, for that matter. But glimpse with me into the world of teens that I see. Let's learn to the extent we can. Today's adolescents look and may act as though they don't care, but they do. Look. Listen. They may act self-sufficient and independent, but they need loads of love, nurturing, and reinforcement. See the differences they face.

Is it harder to be a teen today? Yes.

Is it too easy to be a teen today? Yes.

Our teens have more options, tough choices, and challenges than any previous generation. Adults can be paralyzed by possibilities, but teens are sometimes overwhelmed. Without much experience in decision-making, they face more than they can sort out. The small packets in our wallets when we were teens were Dentyne or Black Jack chewing gum. The small packets today may be crack or a condom.

When I look in our school cafeteria, hundreds of kids look happy and carefree. (Kids around food tend to look that way.) But it's not a carefree generation. Their options, choices, and challenges are before them in a setting unlike any previous generation. Sin has been around since Genesis, chapter 3. But the intensity and impact of evil in this generation is bashing our teens like relentless ocean waves. The world is different and more confusing, and evil is certainly packaged attractively for them.

At the same time that life is tough, it's also too easy to be a young person today. In our country, many teenagers don't have to work to survive. Most have a roof over their head, enough to eat, and seemingly few important or relevant decisions to make on a daily basis. Decisions that matter require accountability. Many of those decisions that matter are made *for* teens today, releasing them from accountability. Life can go on with little effort, and, in fact, with little accountability. Ask adults who grew up in the Depression and they will tell you in lengthy detail just how easy life is today compared to their adolescent years.

Too easy/too hard. Precisely. That's a teen's world.

Different Families/Different Homes

My first-grade reader featured the adventurous family of Dick and Jane. They lived with Mother, Father, Spot the dog, and Ruff the kitten. They played in their neighborhood, spoke to their neighbors, ate with their parents at a round table, and went to school to learn. Growing up in the fifties was likely to be that way.

Forty-two percent of white children today do not live with two parents, and 86 percent of black youngsters will spend most of their lives with one parent. For children born in the eighties, the proportions will increase to 70 percent for white and 94 percent for black children. The average white child spends one-third of his childhood with one parent; the average black child, two-thirds.

Ten different family types are now common, and two-parent families are not the same. Fifty percent of marriages are remarriages, and 60 percent of those end in divorce. Within a few years, more people will live in second-marriage families than first-marriage families.

These statistics represent lots of teenagers adjusting as fast as they can.

> A group of grade-school children were asked to rank what they would miss most if certain things were taken from them. They reported that they would miss TV more than they would their fathers.

A young mother and her fifteen-year-old son sat in my office to register. Her preschool daughter was occupied in the waiting area with a coloring book and crayons. I verified the son's residency papers. Another single woman rented the apartment where they lived. Appropriate papers documented that this family could stay there for the school year. Eric's transferring grades were, you might say, checkered.

We chose classes, toured the school, and visited the school nurse. Eric's mother advised me that she would be difficult to reach because she worked on-site construction and her hours were long. Eric seemed cool, quiet, and confident as I reviewed some school policies and how his first day would begin. He had no questions. He entered the new system and made no waves.

Eric brought his academic habits with him; his school performance continued to be checkered. He was absent a lot. When he started to cut classes, I confronted him. Yes, he would do better, and, yes, he would have his mom call me. (Indeed, she was impossible to reach.)

Mom didn't call, and things got worse. I left a message with her construction supervisor to call the school. She called from a pay phone the next day. She said she had another dime, so would I please talk fast? I had eight minutes. But after one comment, she did the talking. It seemed that Eric was really unhappy in our cold state and wanted to go back to the Southwest. But there was no work for her there, and she could not convince him that she was here to stay.

I questioned Eric.

"But she always moves. I can get her to move home. She just quit her old job because she was going to get married. My little sister's dad can get work for her."

I was getting confused.

"You mean your dad can help her find work in Texas?"

"No. My dad? I don't know my dad. I mean Traci's dad—my little sister's dad. He was okay. He gave me money if he had it. But that didn't work out. We moved in with my uncle and aunt. And then Mom thought she was going to marry this guy with money. She quit her job. But that didn't work out."

"What man are you closest to?" I asked.

"My uncle. I can always go there. When I'm eighteen, I'm goin' there."

Eric had two dads, almost a third, but no father relationship. The grammar-school story of Dick and Jane would have been strange to him. He was not coming to school to learn. He was using school to prove that he didn't belong here, that Mom needed to move back to the place he called home.

As I try to understand the teens with whom I work, statistics help me visualize their lives. Today slightly more than half live with mother or father and siblings. But soon more than half will live in some other type of family. Reconstituted families. Nontraditional families. Stepfamilies. Change has been rapid, and indicators show no slowing of the pace.

Who they live with is changing. What happens where they live is changing equally fast. The adults in the family (whoever they are) have less time for kids. When a child's family shifts from a two-parent family to a one-parent family, the media reminds us that the children usually go with Mom and that her disposable income drops 48 percent. The departing father's disposable income rises 78 percent. These are sad numbers, and money is important. But I've seen kids adjust to this with greater maturity than many adults would.

It is more disturbing to see the poverty of parenting time that kids experience. Just when they need reassurance that the divorce wasn't their fault, assurance that some adult is still committed to them, Dad—or more frequently, Mom—begins working more hours to make ends meet, and is too stressed-out or fatigued to listen.

Two-parent families are not immune from this time crunch. In the majority of two-parent families with adolescents, both parents work. Kids spend less time with adults at home regardless of the family type. In those evening and weekend hours, there are chores to do, bills to pay, groceries to buy. Just surviving can take twenty-four hours a day, seven days a week.

> **In the period between ages ten and fifteen, the amount of time young people spend with their families decreases by half. The bedroom door becomes a significant marker.**

I contrast this to Deuteronomy's description of the inter-action of parents and their children. "And you must think constantly about these commandments I am giving you today. You must teach them to your children and talk about them when you are at home or out for a walk; at bedtime and the first thing in the morning" (Deuteronomy 6:6-7). This sounds like kids were within earshot of an adult much more than now.

I wonder what impact this has on teenagers' knowledge today? I suspect that if they spent more time with caring adults, their knowledge base would be broader and they would have more and better information for making decisions.

I am always curious as to why kids make the decisions they do. So I ask. I requested a conference with Nate. He was being dropped from a class for cutting it five times.

"Nate, we talked about this after the last cut. You understood that you could not cut the class one more time. And you told me it wouldn't happen again. You said you had to work this summer. How are you going to make up this credit?"

"I had no choice." He was too quiet for Nate. I probed.

"I don't think Mr. Ferstein would accept that as a reasonable cause. He would say you chose not to come to his class."

Nate examined his shoes for a long time. Then he looked at me questioningly as if deciding whether to take a big risk.

"I took my girlfriend into the city."

Silence on my part seemed appropriate.

"She had an abortion," he continued in a flat voice. "It was my fault." Then he opened up. They had been going out for a few months. She was fourteen. He really liked her, but they fought a lot. She got pregnant the first time they were intimate.

"My friend said it couldn't happen the first time."

"Did you check out that information with anyone else—like your mom or dad?" I asked.

"We don't talk much." He paused. "We don't talk at all."

The poverty of parenting time in this family left teenagers with few sources of information. Those sources in the area of intimate relationships and sex education weren't very good. A survey of teens ages thirteen to eighteen reported that 76 percent of the boys said parents did not discuss birth control, and 68 percent of the girls said their parents did not discuss "those topics" with them.

Parents often feel that they don't have all the answers. That's okay. Talk anyway. We parents probably know as much as our children's friends. And unlike most of their other information sources, we care about their welfare.

As I talk to teenagers, I see the parenting void being filled by two sources: peers and media. Kids do try to get information. Not just information on *what* and *how,* but also *why.* These answers rub off from who and what they are around, usually peers and media rather than parents. For an increasing number of teens, "peers" means "gang."

These other voices don't need to speak very loudly to be heard. Family noises have been quieted by the time crunch, and many parent voices are feeble. In fact, the parent voice may be silent, as appeared to be the case for one fifteen-year-old boy I counseled.

Phil would not look me in the eye.

"You missed school yesterday," I said softly. "Your mother did not call in."

Silence.

"Does your mom know where you were?" As his high-school counselor, I prodded, needing to know in order to help.

He nodded slightly.

Phil had been in the juvenile detention center for a month. His homecoming did not go smoothly. Coming back to school was worse. His mother was distraught that her good boy had gotten in with the wrong crowd. Teachers saw a changed boy/man. A few of his old friends welcomed him back with open arms—the friends who made his mother shudder.

"Did your mom yell at you?"

He finally looked up.

"Yeah. She's gonna kick me out, Ms. Neff. I got nowhere to go."

A floodgate opened inside and he poured out the stuff going on at home. He was the oldest of four; his mom was doing the best she could to support, nurture, and keep her children in school. She did not understand his sullenness, his outbursts at his little brothers. I don't know whether he followed a leader or desired more than his pocket money could buy. Phil became part of a gang that raided homes. He was arrested, convicted, and sent to the juvenile detention center. After a short time, he was sent home under court supervision.

I listened.

I finally asked a question that had been hanging in the edges of my mind: "What does your father think about all of this?"

"He don't count no more."

Phil's white knuckles and strange voice answered differently. A gate closed inside him. We would talk about Dad later.

Our conversation retreated to safer territory for his emotions for the time being. We talked about how he was doing in his classes. He knew that his teachers' patience was wearing thin. Doing homework was out of the question. It was obvious that his body was in class, but his mind was absent. Phil seldom appeared with paper and pencil, let alone workbook. When teachers tried to talk to him, he might remain silent, confront, or get verbally abusive. You just didn't know how Phil would react.

At a later conference, his mother wept in my office and wrung her ringless, work-worn hands. Phil sat, appearing emotionless, his soft hands folded, a handsome diamond on his little finger. "What happened to you,

Phil?" she wailed. Her heart cry sounded like Socrates, though her culture and life experiences were light years removed from the timeless philosopher:

> *Our youths love luxury. They have bad manners, contempt for authority; they show disrespect for their elders, and love to chatter in place of exercise. Children are now tyrants, not the servants of their household. They no longer rise when their elders enter the room. They contradict their parents, chatter before company, gobble up their food, and tyrannize their teachers.* *

*August Kerber, *Quotable Quotes on Education* (Detroit: Wayne State University Press, 1968), 265.

Phil's mother covered every point the great philosopher did as she cried in frustration! I knew one thing that had "happened" to Phil. He had a dad-shaped void in his gut.

Phil had described to me the months he spent with his father after the divorce. His own three-wheeler, riding on the back of his dad's motorcycle, no school—life with Dad was fun and carefree. Until the truant officer appeared. Then Dad said living with Mom would be best.

After the move, Dad didn't connect with Phil. The few times he said he'd take Phil out, it didn't happen. There were fewer phone calls, and fewer, then none.

"Where is he now?" I asked quietly.

"Like I said, he don't count, and I don't know." But the white-knuckled fists spoke differently.

Our lunch group of educators could have initiated Socrates' statement; it accurately describes the kids in our school today. However, since Socrates said it centuries ago, kids probably haven't changed. However, their world certainly has.

Whether being a teen today is harder or easier than it was for us will never be agreed upon. After we've debated—our generation versus our teens'—we compare ourselves to our parents. And then we compare our parents to our grandparents. And whatever generation is speaking concludes that *they* had it the hardest!

We would keep comparing and debating but the coffee pot runs low, and our middle-aged bodies need to shift from too much sitting. As members of the sandwich generation who are coping with our adolescents and possibly caring for our parents, our days are full, our minds are tired, and sleep must displace debate if we are to face tomorrow's alarm clock. So we agree on one thing: teens' families today are different.

Different Schools

Mr. and Mrs. Carson sank breathlessly onto the seats in my office. Open house was getting the best of them. "How do the kids get to class in just five minutes?"

"Scary, isn't it? I try not to get caught in the halls with a cup of coffee during passing periods." We laughed.

"It wasn't like this when we were in school."

The motion picture industry went on a craze, making movies about how high school was when we were young. Our kids can look at our hairstyles, pony skirts, pink shirts with black pants, pink socks, and white bucks, and laugh. The school cafeteria served meat loaf and mashed potatoes—no choice. We brought dimes to school and slid them in the pockets of our individual United States Savings Bond folders. The teacher put them in her unlocked desk drawer for safekeeping until the next week.

School is different today.

I wish adults could see what school is like for teenagers. Movies like *The Breakfast Club, Teachers,* and *Ferris Bueller's Day Off* misrepresent teachers and administrators. Media expounds our failings and weaknesses. Parents know that schools are not perfect. But there's more that movies don't reveal.

Decades ago, schools were responsible for teaching "Readin', Ritin', and 'Rithmetic." Now we are supposed to teach reading, writing, and arithmetic, plus science, social studies, foreign language, industrial arts, home economics, fine arts (including drama and music), speech, consumer education, health, physical education, career education, and driver education. Our graduates are to be computer literate and prepared for independence with life skills. We are to prevent students from taking drugs, drinking and driving, and committing suicide. Some schools provide free condoms. Some have nursery schools for children of students.

It is not surprising that we don't seem to do anything very well. Excellence in business and industry means sticking to what you're good at or doing a few things well. Schools don't have that luxury—we're supposed to do it all.

There is one benefit for students from this hodgepodge of things that public schools attempt: kids are exposed to a variety of subjects and experiences. They just might find something of interest.

I recall a worried parent of a freshman boy calling me about her son's past unhappiness with school. He was quiet, very tall, and uncoordinated. His glasses were large even for his five-foot-eleven-inch frame. "He hasn't been too happy in junior high, and he's a loner."

Indeed he was. I found him sitting isolated in the cafeteria—a difficult feat when there are probably five hundred kids milling through the fumes of french fries and generic pizza. As we got acquainted, I discovered that he had an intense interest in science. I sent him the school's daily bulletin with an announcement for the Science Club meeting circled. He never stopped by my office to chat, but he would ask brief questions occasionally and began to smile when I saw him in the hall.

Two years later he had found his niche on the Science Olympiad Team as an assistant to two seniors on an egg-drop project. They could drop eggs from the tops of garages or school buildings without the egg breaking, expertise that they demonstrated from the top of the gymnasium, with the local newspaper filming the applauding student body—and the unbroken egg. I watched the team sponsor pat my student on the back. I was applauding that there was a niche for him in our public school.

Because we're trying to teach everything and everybody, public schools do provide lots of variety. The Adventurers Club in our school visits museums, theaters, historic cemeteries, and botanical gardens. The membership is 50 percent Hispanic. Many of them are experiencing our city in a way that they would not have discovered were it not for our school club.

I wish I could say that teenagers' greatest challenges were in the classroom, but recent statistics say that theft and assaults are as frequent in suburban schools as city schools. Kids have to hang onto their stuff and be wary of who knows their locker combination. There may be a pecking order in the cafeteria. It may not be by race. It may be by perceived wealth or popularity. The order may extend to "booking" (knocking a kid's books so they are strewn down the hall) in the hallways and seating at pep rallies. Unfortunately kids seem to be in competition of some sort from the time they hoist their satchel or athletic bag over their shoulder and step on the bus until they return home.

For many teenagers, public school is a place for exposure to new ideas, laboratories, sports, computers, and books that they would not experience elsewhere. They are also required to look out for themselves emotionally and physically. For some teenagers, it is safer than home.

Alicia was usually eating breakfast in the cafeteria when I arrived at school.

"You must get here pretty early," I said.

"Yeah, I come at seven." It became routine to greet her every morning on the way to my office.

One morning she wasn't there. Her friend told me that Alicia had run away. I asked her friend to tell Alicia that I was concerned about her and would like to talk with her.

She met me the next morning at my office door. Her story explained why she preferred to be at school, even at seven o'clock in the morning.

Her mother and stepfather had six children. Both worked evening or night shifts. Alicia was the designated baby-sitter. She was not allowed to date or go to school activities. Her stepdad distrusted any outside influence on this beautiful, tiny girl with large, black eyes. If a phone call came for Alicia, she might get hit. If the children weren't in bed by a designated time, she was in trouble. I asked Alicia why she didn't ask for help. She said she didn't think there was anything anyone could do for her.

"Did he beat you before you left home?" I asked.

"Yes, but that's not why I left. I could take that. I left because . . ." It was as though something stifled her ability to speak. In silence the tears rolled.

I knew. She was safe here.

School is different because our world has changed. Public schools are a microcosm of their societies, communities, and neighborhoods. All those have changed. Kids come in the school doors with different degrees of readiness, preparation, and expectations. Communities provide different resources. Governing bodies assign different tasks. Kids come for different reasons. No wonder school is different.

School is different because the home/school connection is more distant than in previous generations. Fifty-two percent of the parents of fourteen-year-olds have contacted the school regarding their child's academic performance. Forty-nine percent have attended a school meeting, and 28 percent have visited a classroom. I think the statistics are lower for high-school students' parents.

The one-room schoolhouse in the middle of town

across from the church was connected more closely to community families than schools are today. But there is a movement for parents to become more involved in school decisions, board policies, and even retention of administrators. Much would be gained by a closer union of parents and schools. I think that schools would improve, but, more importantly, teenagers and their parents would be brought closer together.

School is different because its hands are tied, literally. If school could be characterized as a person, her hands would be tied behind her back and her mouth taped shut. When a nation removes authority, truth, and accountability from schools, learning cannot take place.

Our teens' schools are different.

Different Work

School consumes seven hours of a teenager's day; sleep supposedly eight. What do kids do with the rest of their time? One-third of them work. They flip hamburgers at fast-food restaurants, bag groceries, stock drugstore shelves, or are cashiers. Pay varies from $4.25 to $6.00 per hour. Positive or negative, teenagers in the marketplace are an increasing part of the employment pie.

Most adults don't object. We'd rather have our teenagers doing something productive, wouldn't we? We worked, didn't we? I drove a tractor on a farm; my husband was a waiter at a family camp and a shoe salesman. We both helped with family gardening, lawn care, and general family chores.

But kids' work is different today. They don't report to their parents or other caring adults known by their family. In fact, when my husband called the drugstore where our son works, the manager was surprised. She said we were the first parents who had contacted her about their child's work.

Our teens' jobs today are usually repetitious with prescribed actions and little opportunity for promotion or new experiences. Employment may or may not be a better option than other activities available to teenagers. Our faculty debates this hotly. We see students sacrifice their studies for monotonous, dead-end jobs. Grades suffer as well as scholarship possibilities. Kids miss out on the opportunity to work on the school newspaper, be a timer at wrestling meets, or create an art masterpiece on the cafeteria window—opportunities that most kids will never again be offered as adults.

Abuses in child-labor laws are increasing. I stopped patronizing one fast-food chain in disgust with how they overworked my students. One boy was responsible for closing the restaurant three school nights each week. When he asked to work only on weekends, he was fired.

Sometimes kids don't object to hours that violate the guidelines. Most have as many ways to spend money as adults do. Many support a "life-style." Some save for college, but most, according to one poll, buy clothing and food. They get a job to get a car, then they have to keep the job because they have the car. The truth is that teenage consumerism is much like adult consumerism. One researcher found that teens who work more than fifteen to twenty hours a week tend to spend less time with their parents than their nonworking classmates. They are more likely to daydream in class, have more behavior problems, and are more likely to drink and smoke cigarettes and marijuana.*

*Annetta Miller, "Work and What It's Worth," *Newsweek,* June 1990, 33.

There is at least one advantage to adolescents working. Getting a job heads the list for topics on which teenagers want their parents' advice. Drugs are at the bottom of the list. Holding a job provides a preview for teenagers of an adult's world—negotiating salaries, juggling work schedules, and getting along with bosses. When teenagers work, the experience can be common ground for teen-parent communication.

Different Play

Remember driving around the A & W, and driving around again, and driving around again? That was big time recreation in Worthington, Indiana on a hot summer's Saturday night. Eventually you would pull up to the curb or, better yet, back up to the fence so you could see the circling cars and not have to leave after forty-five minutes. Saturday night recreation has changed. Many teens have access to cars but, instead of cruising, they drive to the mall, or to somebody's house for a party.

I took an informal survey of what teens like to do with their spare time. The most frequent answer, regardless of sex or group affiliation, was, "hang out." This means "be with other people you like." What is important is who you're with, not where you are. But the place has to "let it happen" (whatever "it" is). A mall may be the perfect setting if you want to meet kids from other schools or shop. A home is preferable if you are into music. You don't "hang out" at school. You might go there for a game or variety show—you hang out afterward. Few restaurants meet the criterion. (Managers call "hanging out" loitering.) Homes are good for video games, watching movies, eating, and talking.

> **If you always do what you've always done,**
> **you'll always get what you've always got.**

In my informal survey, teens fell into two categories. Over half said they had practically no time for "hanging out" and were happy that way. These were the teens with jobs or who were involved in school activities or church-related organizations. About 30 percent had time to do what they wanted and were sometimes bored.

I asked what they had enjoyed most in the last year. I was delightfully surprised by one common answer. Our community had been flooded. Streets were closed; houses had first floors under water. Some were spared by sandbag dikes hastily thrown up. Many students' most enjoyable experience was helping neighbors and the community during those weeks. It was more fun than hanging out! (I wonder if Socrates knew that side of his students?)

There is a dangerous side to teens' play today. For many, having fun means "party." For many, "party" means available alcohol and possibly drugs. The combination becomes deadly because of the alcohol-sex connection. When their inhibitions are dulled with alcohol, teens do what they've seen thousands of times on TV and in movies. That accounts for the fact that 40 percent of our teenage girls experience pregnancy.

Today's teens live in a dangerous world. It is incredibly different from our world as teens. Though as adults and parents we may struggle to understand and find common ground with our teens, I am comforted by this thought: As different as teens are today, I am reminded that they were wired by my Creator. And he made them in his image. God created parents in his image also—including me. Different temperaments? Yes. Different schools, different work, different play, different worlds? For sure! But we share the same Creator—a bond we can build on. This knowledge gives me the courage and desire to get to know adolescents better. We'll talk about understanding and knowing our teens in the next chapter. It is possible; we're from the same Maker. There is hope that we can know and love them, because God made them.

— 3 —

Mismatched: When You
and Your Teen Don't Fit

Thirty twelve- and thirteen-year-olds collected in our basement for our son's birthday party. While taking coats, I observed four-foot-ten-inch boys walking tall, who smiled at me with dimples and twinkling eyes, the impish grin of childhood. One tall, thin young man hardly glanced at me. "Please don't ask me a question or I'll blush," was written all over his face. The immense physical contrasts were matched with differences in how much self-confidence they emoted and differences in communication.

Contrasts in the girls were just as great. Some were tiny and could play a nine-year-old movie role. Others looked all of seventeen, dressed the part, and wore carefully chosen and applied makeup. Long, permed, and almost blonde hair seemed to predominate. I sensed lots of hours had gone into "getting ready." Some walked in confidently like the party was theirs. Others refused to enter except enveloped in their group.

God seemed to have gone overboard on diversity when he created adolescents! These teens were different at birth. Some lay quietly in their hospital cubicles, the world oblivious to their existence. Others grabbed for the world's attention from the moment of birth. They howled for food, howled when wet, howled when bored, and just howled to howl. Thirteen years later the contrasts seem greater.

How could these contrasting human beings have enough in common to spend over three hours at Robb's party together? (Okay. So I not only wondered, I worried!) On one of my frequent trips to refill the ice bowl, I was privileged to glimpse one of those unforgettable events that convince you that God has truly created each human being differently. The stage was set by the DNA that mysteriously contain physical traits, personality bent, and potentials for mind and body.

Our trampoline became the party theater. Each teen took a turn, ran, and leaped on that thing, their creativity, personality, and skills exploding, often with a hoot or screech to match their leap or fall. One girl nimbly did two complete flips in midair and landed precisely with confident upturned palms and a gleaming braces smile. One boy could manage to get his body only a foot or so into the air (his weight was progressing ahead of his strength). He earned his applause, however, by doubling into a ball before he spilled onto the carpet rolling about five kids down like bowling pins. The game was a tribute to the myriad of contortions of which the human body is capable. Each one received applause, whistles, and shrieks.

Different.

It's fun to sit back and observe God's creativity and sense of humor when he created adolescents; that is, if you're looking at somebody else's kids. It's not so much fun when it's your teen, and you don't understand the difference, or you don't appreciate his individuality, or you just can't believe how he got wired up!

Sometimes you think how he is wired is okay—for some other family. You're just mismatched.

Research has finally documented what we parents have known all along. Stella Chess studied significant differences in disposition from birth into the adult years. From her findings she identified categories of temperament that are measurably different from birth: activity level, predictability, approach/withdrawal, adaptability, sensory threshold, quality of mood, intensity of reactions, distractibility, persistence, and attention span. As her longitudinal study evolved, she noted that temperament was consistent from infancy. We already knew it, didn't we? Our kids' temperaments are different.

She also documented that adjustment for the adolescent was not dependent solely on the individual's temperament, but also the temperaments of his or her family members, and what she called "goodness of fit." When parents' demands and expectations are compatible with the teen's temperament, abilities, and other characteristics, there is a match. Chess summarized the ten categories of temperamental attitudes to the three types: the difficult child, the easy child, and the slow-to-warm-up child.

Her volumes of statistics support what experienced parents have known: genetics and environment interact and an adolescent emerges. This happens in a family—a family system with different degrees of goodness of fit. She described the resulting family combinations as follows:

- calm child plus calm parent = heaven in the home
- hyper child plus calm parent = survival
- calm child plus hyper parent = survival
- hyper child plus hyper parent = heaven help the family fireworks

Different infants grow into different adolescents. Let's take this fact a step further. Those different adolescents grow into different adults who become parents who create families with different infants. No wonder fireworks can result in some family combinations!

Many parents were trained to believe that they shaped and molded their child and therefore could produce whatever they chose or the best they were able to do. Carried to a logical conclusion, this would mean that the parent would create the adolescent. Stimulus-response. Kids are what you make them.

Most of today's parents learned that philosophy. The problem: it is wrong because God and his creative act are left out. That philosophy gives parents more credit or more guilt than they deserve. During every year of life, environment shapes a child, but it never removes differences in the genetic code. An aggressive, active infant can become a razor-sharp lawyer, a linebacker, a high-income drug dealer, or a camp director. We can talk about environment, and we will. But we have spent too little time learning about inherent, inborn, God-instilled differences and how those differences affect our parenting.

I believe that many teen crises begin with a mismatch between them and significant others in their lives *and/or* stress events that they are not equipped to handle. Sometimes the characteristics of a parent and teen are naturally irritating to each other. Family stress events bring out differences.

Dear parent, before you decide that this author is going to begin parent-bashing, let me remind you that at one time my four children were all teens. With our particular combination of "born to us" and adopted children, the differences and mismatches were sometimes extreme. Let's look together at the combinations that can escalate normal stresses of life to crises; normal "stretching for independence" to defiance.

The mismatch may not be in the family. It may be in the school, the neighborhood, the extended family, or the community. The mismatch may result in misunderstandings, defiance, or a big-time crisis for the teen and everyone around him or her. Parents may be unable to transform a mismatch or prevent stress events. But parents may be able to avoid or soften crises. A significant beginning is to . . .

- Know your teen.
- Recognize risk factors in your teen.

• Check your teen's life-stress events.

Let's examine each of these areas in detail.

Know Your Teen

Gary Smalley and John Trent created a Personal Strengths Inventory that is helpful in knowing your teen. It has many uses, but for our purposes, let's look at their summaries for how people are bent. Their categories are similar to Stella Chess's combinations of temperamental attitudes. A difficult child is called a *lion;* an easy child is either a *beaver* or an *otter;* and a slow-to-warm-up child is called a *golden retriever.*

Characteristics for Each Type of Child

Lion	Takes charge	Bold
	Determined	Purposeful
	Assertive	Decision Maker
	Firm	Leader
	Enterprising	Goal-driven
	Competitive	Self-reliant
	Enjoys challenges	Adventurous
Beaver	Deliberate	Discerning
	Controlled	Detailed
	Reserved	Analytical
	Predictable	Inquisitive
	Practical	Precise
	Orderly	Persistent
	Factual	Scheduled
Otter	Takes risks	Fun-loving visionary
	Motivator	Enjoys change
	Energetic	Creative
	Very verbal	Group-oriented
	Promoter	Mixes easily

	Avoids details	Optimistic
	Likes variety	
Golden retriever	Loyal	Adaptable
	Nondemanding	Sympathetic
	Even keel	Thoughtful
	Avoids conflict	Nurturing
	Enjoys routine	Patient
	Dislikes change	Tolerant
	Deep relationships	Good listener

Teens come in all shapes, sizes, and types, just as parents do. Which category best describes your teen? Which one describes you? You may see the source of fireworks simply in how your teen is wired—and you, too.

I hurriedly climbed into my teenage son's car for a quick trip to the grocery store. His car was nicknamed "The Beast"—for good reason. Now this son, a golden retriever by temperament, is a technical, quiet person who loves to putter with mechanical stuff. I did not notice that the radio was askew, and a few other items were precariously attached to the lower dash. As I backed out of the garage, I also forgot that this car did not shift from park to reverse, or reverse to drive; it lurched. (Maybe it was tired, like I was, and afraid to move in low gear or it would fall asleep!)

I glanced in the rearview mirror out of habit and shifted into reverse. The Beast lurched back out of the garage and then lunged forward. At my feet lay an electronic mass that looked like lightning had hit an electronic jackpot. A radio, an equalizer, and a makeshift CD player were "minutes" away from being secured to transform the Beast into a moving concert hall of the purest quality. I did not see the makings of a sound system at my feet. I saw a mess!

I wish I could say that I waxed philosophical and quietly contemplated how differently my son and I are designed, how patient he is working on his projects. I wish I had reminded myself of our different temperaments that have naturally led to different priorities in our lives. Instead I extracted my feet and rushed into the house to call for help from John. You may have accurately guessed that I am a lion. Irritated at the delay and worried that some expensive gadget was broken, I half listened to his explanation of the marvel he was creating.

"Is it drivable?" Somehow, all that mess meant to me that the engine might not work, and my trip would be delayed. My three teenage sons thought my question was humorous. I did not.

Looking back, that little slice of life was a caricature of how different John's temperament is from mine. We're wired differently to begin with by our Creator. Then our living experiences widen the variation. It's no wonder that we often don't see eye-to-eye, or heart-to-heart, or even voice-to-ear.

Some types of teens are more likely to be at the center of fireworks, if not the cause. You may have known when you read Dr. Dobson's *The Strong-Willed Child* that you were in for excitement. And sure enough, your little pistol is now a big pistol—except louder and more confrontive than you could have imagined. You may have been told by the school that your grade-schooler would probably be an adult mover and shaker.

But it's teen time. And you don't appreciate her practicing on your home and family.

Getting to know your teens and accepting the fact that God-given characteristics can become God-blessed strengths can help you parent your teens and help them through crises.

Recognize Risk Factors in Your Teen

There are a number of "risk" factors that we can observe in our teens. (I must quickly add that we should also recognize "risk" factors in ourselves. We'll discuss those in chapter 13.) We can reduce stress and risk where possible and at least learn to accept those factors that cannot be changed.

I found myself becoming angry at one son who hibernated at large family gatherings. As I thought about his personality and shyness, I recognized that he didn't dislike his relatives, and he wasn't purposefully trying to irritate his mother. He just found those gatherings stressful. His younger brother thought they were fun parties! But for my shy son, the situation was a mismatch for his personality.

We were able to compromise. He was comfortable in the crowd if he had specific tasks to focus on such as gathering chairs or pouring pop. I was comfortable with him retreating for a specific time period if he would mix part of the time.

Give yourself the following quiz about your teenager. I asked my son if he would answer the questions and we could compare answers. We had lots of laughs at some of my guesses. I didn't know him as well as I thought. But I know him better now.

How Well Do You Know Your Teenager?

1. Who is your teen's best friend?
2. What color would he/she like for the walls in his/her bedroom?
3. Who is your teen's greatest hero?
4. What embarrasses your teen most?
5. What is your teen's biggest fear?
6. What is his/her favorite type of music?
7. What person outside the immediate family has most influenced the life of your teen?
8. What is his/her favorite school subject?
9. What is his/her least favorite school subject?
10. What has your teen done that he/she feels most proud of?
11. What is your teen's biggest complaint about the family?
12. What sport does your teen most enjoy?
13. What is his/her favorite TV program?
14. What really makes your teen angry?
15. What would your teen like to be when he/she grows up?
16. What chore does your teen like least?
17. What three foods does your teen like most?
18. What is your teen's most prized possession?
19. What is his/her favorite family occasion?
20. What activity did your teen enjoy most last weekend?

Knowing your teen will help you recognize his or her risk factors, and you may be able to pinpoint where fireworks can be lit. Carrie and her mom would have profited from taking this quiz together. When you as a parent see risk situations and characteristics that fit poorly, you have a head start on avoiding crises or at least coping with fireworks in the best way possible.

Check Your Teen's Life-Stress Events

The "stuff" in teens' lives can be incredible. Life-stress events can push a teen who copes with most things beyond his or her limits. As adults, we can look back and say that growing up is a stress test—preparation for the big stress test of life (parenting!). During the teen years, an important developmental task is to learn coping skills for life's difficulties. Kids aren't born with those skills; they only learn them by living. Parents can't spare children difficulties or loan them their skill kit. But we can recognize the situations and react appropriately because we recognize the stress.

Stress Events*

Points ...... Stress
100 .... Parent dies
73 .... Parents divorce
65 .... Parents separate
63 .... Parent travels as part of job
63 .... Close family member dies
53 .... Individual has illness or injury
50 .... Parent remarries
47 .... Parent fired from job
45 .... Parents reconcile
45 .... Mother goes to work
44 .... Family member has change in health
40 .... Mother becomes pregnant
39 .... Individual has difficulties at school
39 .... Sibling is born

39 .... Individual has a school readjustment (new
teacher or class)
38 .... Family's financial condition changes
37 .... Close friend has an injury or illness
36 .... Individual starts or changes extracurricular
activity (music lessons, etc.)
35 .... Number of fights with siblings changes
31 .... Individual is threatened by violence at school
30 .... Individual has personal possessions stolen
29 .... Responsibilities at home change
29 .... Older brother or sister leaves home
29 .... Individual has trouble with grandparents
28 .... Individual has outstanding personal achievement
26 .... Individual moves to another city
26 .... Individual moves to another part of town
25 .... Individual receives or loses a pet
24 .... Personal habits change
24 .... Individual has trouble with teacher
20 .... Individual moves to a new house
20 .... Individual changes to a new school
19 .... Individual vacations with family
18 .... Friends change
17 .... Individual attends camp
16 .... Sleeping habits change
15 .... Number of family get-togethers changes
15 .... Eating habits change
12 .... Individual has a birthday party

*David Elkind, *The Hurried Child* (Reading Mass.: Addison
Wesley Publishing Company, 1981), 162-163.

From my perspective as a high-school counselor, the
potential for stress in teens' lives is increasing. Teens
move with greater frequency, families are shifting and
restructuring, gang activity is increasing threats of violence. In fact, most of these stress items are not static in
our environment. They are growing.

Additionally, this stress test does not include teen
pregnancy, physical or sexual abuse, date rape, or other
catastrophic situations that are real for some teens. Events

that previously belonged on the adult stress test are now factors for teens. Getting a job or being fired from a job may be the teen's personal situation, not his or her parents'.

If you see a stress event, acknowledge it. Your teen will be comforted by just this simple statement. "Moving (or whatever the stress event may be) must be rough on you. You're in a tough situation." In my work, I've concluded that parents can't know how their teen feels in stress events. But parents can acknowledge their teen's feelings and validate them.

If we want to be helpful to teens in stress, we must acknowledge and confront the issues and then discuss them as family, not adversaries.

For some reason, teens often react to stress with defiance. Parents react to teen defiance with anger. Parent anger increases the teen's stress. The circle doesn't end. The teen's behavior escalates. Parents' anger increases, and a stressful situation that could be avoided may create additional family fireworks.

Here are some parent tools to reduce defiance.

Acknowledge that you recognize what your teen is feeling. It's all right to be angry about a move or a divorce. Just as parents have a right to their feelings, so do teens.

Define acceptable behavior. Anger because of a move is okay. Being truant from school is not. In a two-parent family, agree on what "acceptable" behavior is. Otherwise the "but she said" game will become your teen's theme song.

Define consequences for unacceptable behavior.

Since we will look at specific consequences in later chapters, I will summarize a few important facts and common problems.

Teens, like children and some adults, will test, so make sure that *you* are sure what *unacceptable* is. Be prepared with strength and patience to enforce consequences.

One father insisted that his son go to school—after an accumulation of multiple tardies and ten days of truancy. He announced his order to me by phone and then proceeded with his life as usual. He left his house early for work and was unavailable by phone until 6:00 P.M. His son proceeded with his life as usual—sleeping in and sporadically attending school.

Next his father announced that he would take his son's car keys if he missed another day of school. When the next truancy occurred, Dad decided that the inconvenience of a son without car keys upset Dad's life-style. I would guess that his son's fireworks were also "inconvenient." His son dropped out of school.

This father did not enforce consequences; therefore, they were ineffective. To be effective, consequences must be immediate, specific, and consistent. As I look back, I can see that the same principles that are successful in parenting young children work with teenagers. It's easy to relax on the principles too soon because we are looking at such a grown-up looking person. But no matter how grown-up teens appear to be, they still seem to thrive with immediate, specific, and consistent consequences.

For example, the "time-out" technique of sitting in isolation and thinking is a helpful tool with young teens.

If they have exploded or have used inappropriate language, sitting ten minutes to think will reduce the likelihood of that happening again. Repeated explosions earn longer "time-outs."

Another helpful tool is "write about it." Your teen's ticket to getting out of the time-out chair might be two pages on "Why name-calling is inappropriate" or "How I would feel if . . ."

Establish incentives for appropriate behavior. Possible incentives would include:

- Freedom on weekends is dependent on average or higher weekly accumulative grades
- Money for an entertainment event on the weekend is dependent on completing family jobs and responsibilities by noon on Saturdays
- Use of a vehicle is dependent on driving it legally and safely
- Use of a family vehicle is dependent on being a team player, a positive part of the family, not fireworks

Teens are more likely to accept parents' answers if the facts are laid out. Incentives at the Neff house might sound like this:

"Robb, I won't have the energy left to supervise your sleep-over if I've had to police bickering brothers all evening beforehand."

"Charles, I will have no motivation to take you to the skate shop if I've had to repeatedly remind you of your family jobs."

In my counseling experience, I've discovered that few adults can suggest rewards or consequences that are effective for another parent's child. However, by communicating with others—other parents, people who work with teens, other teens, or your own teens—most parents can discover effective consequences and rewards.

Many families find parent/teen contracts effective tools for reducing fireworks. A contract states what each person will (or will not) do for a specific period of time or in a specific set of circumstances.

One family frequently got tangled in "blaming" arguments when they disagreed. This escalated to fireworks that created more anger than the original disagreement. The family made a contract that when either party recognized "blaming" in the conversation they would give a time-out hand signal. Conversation would stop—even if Dad was talking. Blaming had to stop and the conversation was to go on track toward a solution.

Our bias for incentives may be to reward with things. Supposedly that's the American way. In my experience and work, however, I've seen teens respond more to incentives of special events, trips with special people, and freedom that gives them the opportunity to choose.

With sadness I recognize that those of us who help teens in crisis have a growing challenge ahead of us. The stress events in our teens' lives are increasing. With empathy, I believe that parenting teens will be increasingly demanding, possibly more frustrating. However, with hope, I believe that parents will rise to the challenge.

We need to know our teens better than previous generations knew theirs. I believe we will need to be on greater alert to our teens' individual risk factors. We need to be in touch with the stress events in their lives. And we need to be nonjudgmental about teens' differences.

Perhaps you as a parent do not struggle with being judgmental. I have worked with many parents who do. When I look in the mirror, I see one of them. Since I am a lion by temperament, I am goal-driven. I value speed and quickly leap to solutions. I am matched with a golden-retriever teen who is patient, tolerant, and dislikes change. I am sorry to have to admit that I have judged my son and put our differences under right and wrong categories. And guess who I always think is right!

Temperament differences are not right/wrong issues. They are God-given. In our humanness, we want to rank everything into good, better, best, *or* fair, poor, or the pits. In fact, we can even make these differences moral issues. Teens lose when we judge them for their temperament differences. They feel rejected and lonely. We'll look at this again in the chapter on self-esteem.

Parents lose because we risk forfeiting the great privilege of liking our teen. It's hard to like someone you've judged. It's difficult for the friendship dimension of parenting to grow if our teen feels our disapproval.

Different is not wrong.

As children we sang "Jesus loves the little children." We gave loud assent to God's diversity in creating people. Parenting teens gives us the opportunity to live as adults, to live what we believe.

— 4 —

What's a Family For?

A teen is in crisis. That teen is not alone. Somewhere, at some time, family existed: a mom, a dad, kids, a grandma, or an uncle. You may be reading this book because you're part of that young person's family. If that is the case, no one needs to explain to you that a teen in crisis does not suffer alone. You know it!

You feel the fear. The tension wraps around your nerve endings like a python. Sometimes you think you can touch sadness when you step in your front door. Crisis for teens is never an island experience.

Family is increasingly the stage of the crisis, the place where the fireworks erupt. That's because family is the last frontier, the last place, the last institution where people have to be We's, not Me's.

The Golden Era of Me has prevailed for many years. What do *I* want? What's good for *me?* Are *my* rights being honored? I, Me, Mine. I did it my way; I'm proud of it, and the world applauds my individualism. The Golden Era of Greed has been the companion of the Golden Era of Me.

The supreme teaching of society has been personal satisfaction, personal success, and individual rights. Television teaches Me-ism, as does our government, and our judicial system. Our schools have clamored onto the bandwagon. It's easy to climb on. Everything in us shouts, "Yes! Yes!"

> **Family is where people learn WE, not just ME.**

Problem. Family is We.

Family is more than individuals sharing the same space, using the same microwave, and depending on a twenty-gallon water heater. In families people share the toothpaste, air space, and gas tanks.

When teens go to school, they have to look out for themselves. They have to compete to survive.

When they turn the key and enter their homes, competition creates fireworks, and looking out for themselves offends others. What works outside hurts the family. Me has to give way to We.

No wonder it's tough to be a parent. You are the only person left to teach your kids one of life's most important lessons: How to get along with others.

Where else are kids taught to respect others' property, delay personal gratification for the benefit of others, or take care of people who can't care for themselves? Even if you are not consciously and actively teaching your teen those lessons, you are their teacher/role model simply by the fact that both of you are living at the same address, in the same space.

I treasure a mental picture that illustrates this fact. Recently our family returned from vacation. On the way home, we stopped at the train station so that our twenty-year-old daughter, who now lives in another state, could catch her train home. Bob and I stood inside looking out at the tracks, watching our daughter surrounded by her brothers. It was a poignant moment. Happiness for her independence, sadness to see her go, and thankfulness for the week together, jumbled inside and pushed my heart up into my throat. Then these four children began playing an old game that they've played since they were big enough to bump into each other. Each one takes a few steps toward another and then jumps sideways into brother or sister bumping, or sometimes pounding shoulders in midair. They have done this on the ground, in swimming pools, on trampolines, and everywhere for years. In front of the train station, oblivious to their audience, they were leaping at each other, laughing, and bouncing off each other. Sometimes the collisions were between two, three, and sometimes all four.

The train's shrill whistle abruptly halted their game. Big sister and big brother soul-hugged. Younger brothers hugged tentatively. We raced for luggage, gave quick kisses, and exchanged "Be carefuls". And she was gone.

Family. The place where people bump shoulders. Collide. Learn to be We.

A big, black, baggy, *clean* shirt is on the washing machine. But it's my brother's. He's not here; he's left for school. But I may not wear it. A lesson in We.

It's 11:30 P.M. I love my music. I love my music loud. My sound system sounds better at high decibels. But my parents are sleeping. If I blare my music now and my father's alarm goes off at 5:00 A.M. for him to go to work, Dad will be tired with the right to be hostile. A lesson in We.

Teachers of Me-ism	Peers
	Government
	Judicial system
	Newspapers
	Television
	Radio
	School
	Athletics (most)
	Business
	Media advertising
Lessons of Me-ism	Them against us
	Individual prosperity
	Self-centered leadership
	Individual rights
	Don't get caught
	Cutting up others is funny
	Entertain yourself
	Achieve at any cost
	Win at any cost
	End justifies means
	Faster is better
	Strong is good/Weak is bad
	Expose the bizarre
	Moderation is boring
	Take everything to the limit
	Sexuality is public domain
	Superficial relationships
Teachers of We-ism	Family

Lessons of We-ism	Kinship—get close
	Delay gratification
	Self-restraint
	Modest sexuality
	Respect others' property
	Respect others' rights
	Care for those in need
	Care for the helpless
	Accountable leadership

In my counseling position I sense a common emotion in parents. Increasingly parents of teens are afraid. We feel that we are the only ones who are trying to lead and guide in a direction that matters to no one else. In fact, all other forces seem to be pushing and pulling our teens the opposite direction. Dear parent, your feelings are valid. You feel fear, and you feel lonely.

Perhaps looking at the chart above helps you understand why you feel that way. Family is the only teacher left on the "We" list.

Today, most parents feel inadequate and insecure about their ability to parent. I grew up believing that the majority was probably right. In our classrooms the teacher would ask, "Who believes answer X is right? Who believes answer Y is right?" If mine was the only hand up, I figured I was wrong.

And now I'm a parent.

Parents question their decision making. Parents question their priorities. Parents question their values. And while we're pondering and questioning, our teens are being steered downstream by the majority. And we're supposed to be providing stable, consistent leadership! It's a tough job!

Don't give up. You're doing many things right.

Learning to Be "We" When There's No Crisis

Families should be teaching "We" before the crises arise. How?

Be family. Just by living together, learning to compromise, and learning to cooperate, accommodate, and negotiate, you are living something wonderful and important. You are providing your teen the most appropriate setting, the best place to learn life's most important lessons. Lay aside false guilt, acknowledge that your job is tough, and pat yourself on the back.

Make room for your teen to be a teen. The Chinese word for independence is *jiritsu.* It combines two Chinese characters. One contains the idea of self, the other, the idea of standing. Teens must learn to stand by themselves as they move toward independence.

For a teenage self to stand alone, the teen has to decide if the values that he has been taught will become his, or if he will acquire and internalize different values. He has to test standing alone in different circumstances, some of which are risky. Teens will challenge a lot of their parents' teachings. Lions will challenge with a different intensity than golden retrievers. A calm teen challenges differently than a difficult teen.

This is a good time to remember our "goodness-of-fit" principle. Depending on your temperament and your teen's temperament, her/his *jiritsu* will affect the entire family differently.

Watch for danger signals. Two important signals are isolating oneself and changing drastically.

Arguing is a normal way for a young person to sort himself from family and test his ability to stand. The problem comes when the challenge goes beyond arguing. When a teen feels that he can no longer argue, he may pull away and isolate. That is a danger signal. When the family lines of communication totally break, a crisis may be brewing.

Arguing is a good signal. (Dear parent, I know you sighed heavily when I said that.) It shows that your teen feels she can still come to you to test her different ideas. It shows that he believes you'll be there for him to push against. On many topics you will give your teen a different perspective, one that he or she will get nowhere else.

Some parents don't have much energy or are unwilling to invest it in taking care of their young person. Carrie's father was losing his energy to alcohol and to business travel. Arguing takes energy. As a mother, I think feeding, diapering, and bathing my children took less energy than arguing does now. I often don't feel I have the energy, and I may have to say, "Let's talk about it in the morning. I'm not very rational right now."

When parents can see arguing as a valuable investment rather than a personal put-down, teens are less likely to isolate and crises are less likely to occur.

Drastic change is another signal that needs to be heeded. Parents have to make some careful calls because teens are constantly changing. We are in the delicate position of trying to determine what is a drastic change and what is normal adolescent, up/down personality experimentation.

> "Don't laugh at a youth for his affectations; he is only trying on one face after another to find his own."
> —Logan Pearsall Smith

As a parent, I understand how hard it is to keep up with teens' changes. One of our sons loved the shaved-head look for a season. Another seemed to develop an allergy to a barber's chair for three years. Teens try on faces and personalities as they search for self.

How does a parent distinguish between normal and drastic? If your teen does something that makes you say, "That's not my kid," the signal has been given.

If your son who usually is an arguer suddenly takes a swing at you or becomes violent with other family members, he's signaling. If your daughter who has been a people person since infancy begins isolating for hours in her room, she's sending a signal. You don't need to turn into an undercover agent to see the signals. Just keep your eyes open. This list should help you identify your teen's signals for help.

Signals

1. Changes in work or school attendance
2. Changes in quality of work, grades, or discipline
3. Withdrawal from responsibility
4. General changes in overall attitude
5. Unusual flare-ups or outbreaks of temper
6. Deterioration of physical appearance and grooming

7. Turning away from former friends and activities
8. Stealing from family, employer, or school
9. Reduced motivation, self-discipline, or self-esteem
10. Change in sleep habits

What's a family for? Because you share the same space with your teen, you may be the first to see the signal. In fact, you may be the only one who sees the signal.

Helping professionals love the word "intervention." The dictionary defines "to intervene" this way: "to come in or between by way of hindrance or modification." Teens who are signaling trouble need someone to intervene, someone or something to change their direction, moving them away from crisis. Family can be that something or someone who intervenes.

What Parents Can Do When They See Danger Signals

How can families intervene? I sit with parents in my office when their teens are signaling trouble. "What can I do?" Sometimes they ask with hopelessness, sometimes in anger, sometimes in desperation.

My first answer—and I say this to myself as well—is talk, communicate, talk, communicate, talk, communicate, and talk some more. Teens need to know that it's all right to disagree or to express an opinion. If they are not allowed to communicate their feelings at home, they may not express their opinion in peer groups either, and will end up just following the crowd. Family is a place to develop strong communication skills. Family is the place to talk.

Carrie's day at school was quite different from her parents' memories of school days. We parents need to realize that growing up these days is more complicated than when we were young. Choices have larger and sometimes more devastating consequences. Teens are usually dying to talk to someone about important topics and choices, including love, sex, and pregnancy—topics that parents feel hesitant about bringing up.

Sometimes people who *will* talk with our teens about these topics have different values than we do. That's why parents *should* talk about these important topics. We parents may have to be the initiators, listen a lot, and hear things we don't want to hear. How we respond may determine whether our teenager keeps talking.

When my teen tells me she's doing something I don't want her to do, I may want to jump in and tell her why it's not acceptable. If I quietly listen longer, I may learn the reasons for her behavior.

An important point of adolescence—some experts say the *whole* point—is to find ways that teens can set themselves apart from their parents. While your teen is shopping around for ways to exercise *jiritsu*, it's easy to become critical of him or her. When teens sense that parents are rejecting *them*, family has lost the ability to intervene.

Tips on Communicating

1. Start by asking "safe" questions.
   "How are things going?"
   "How are your friends doing these days?"

---

2. **Ask open-ended questions.**
   Don't just accept, "Fine."
   Explore "how" and "why."
   "How did that paper turn out?"

3. **Include positives.**
   "Thanks for calling to tell me you'd be late."
   "One thing I appreciate about you is . . ."

4. **Be honest.**
   "It really scares me when . . ."
   "I don't know, but I'll help you find out."
   "Here's my opinion and why."

5. **Listen—actively listen.**
   Ask for clarification if you are unsure about
       what you are hearing.
   "Is this what you're saying?"
   "I didn't know that's how you felt."

6. **Communicate acceptance of your teen whether or
   not you agree with or understand his/her position.**

What's a family for? Communicating.

When parents ask, "What can I do?" my second answer is: establish guidelines. I hear teens tell their parents that they want more guidelines. (My children probably wish I hadn't heard kids make that request in my office. I come home with too many ideas!) This is a common answer and one that you have heard before, but I repeat it for six important reasons. I see parents:

1. doubting their ability to set guidelines
2. relinquishing their role as parents
3. too busy to prioritize this parental responsibility
4. afraid of alienating their teen

5. unsure of their own values
6. ashamed of their own weaknesses

I see these six reasons and a few more when I look in the mirror! Our fears can make our tough task even more difficult. We can hesitate to set guidelines when our teen is signaling desperately.

A young person is likely to have had sixty-eight teachers by the time he or she graduates from high school. Each teen has watched 19,656 hours of television and movies, browsed through a two-story house height of magazines, and listened to the lyrics of songs for 4,914 hours. He or she may have had countless coaches and heard numerous assembly speakers and newscasts. But you are the only parents that your children have. You may feel inadequate, uninformed, and scared, but you're the best they've got.

(And, by the way, nobody is competing for your job! No one wants to take your place—even when you wish someone would! Someone may want to use your teen, but no one else wants to parent him! No one else wants *that* responsibility!)

Today's teens have so many choices. They feel stress; they feel pressure from the sheer volume of choices to make. When parents provide a framework, it's easier for teens to make the smaller decisions within that framework.

A single mother sat in my office at her daughter's side. The tears rolled. Sunny was in trouble academically. Mom had been letting her make her own choices about going out on school nights. But her choosing days were over. Mom laid down the rule: no more going out Sunday night through Thursday night until the next marking period with all passing grades. Then they would talk about it.

Sunny listened as her mother talked and wept about having a baby before she graduated. Sunny heard her mom's fears for Sunny's future. Mom listened to Sunny's fears, too.

After her mother left my office, Sunny turned to me and said, "Life's easier when somebody tells you what's expected of you." Lots of teens feel that way but are afraid to say it, or they think that no one will listen.

Parents can set guidelines for the family. The framework they set expresses their expectations. We can set guidelines through discussion and compromise. Curfew, using the car, and dating are examples.

We can set other guidelines through parental wisdom. Declaring your home a smoke-free environment is a guideline set by parental wisdom. I have a friend whose husband died of lung cancer when their daughter was eighteen. As a little girl, Sonja had pleaded with her dad not to smoke; as a teen, she followed his footsteps. In her time of grief, my friend declared that her home would be smoke-free. Sonja sat cross-legged on the sidewalk and smoked, walked the dog and smoked, went to work and smoked. Setting the guideline was an important step, and not an easy one, for my friend to take.

Just for communication's sake, take the following list and write each item on separate index cards. If there are four people in your family in the teen and parent category, write each item on four cards. Give each teen and parent a set of index cards. Label three shoe boxes: one "teen decision," one "teen/parent compromise," and one "parental wisdom." Each person should initial each of the cards and drop them in the appropriate box.

curfew
sleep-overs
weekend activities
music
parentless parties
movie choices
drugs
no sex till marriage
bedtime
booze
smoke-free environment
entertainment
church involvement
school-related activities

If you are hesitant to put these topics on cards for family discussion, consider that in health class and possibly social studies, English, and speech, the topics include abortion, homo- and bisexuality, and euthanasia.

After everyone has sorted, communicate. (Remember numbers 5 and 6 on the "Tips on Communicating" chart!)

Later you may want to add abortion, sexual orientation, euthanasia, pregnancy, and other topics that are important to you or your teens.

If you find communicating a stretching and sometimes painful exercise, look at the lighter side: a healthy dose of humor goes a long way. We educators have a thirteen-point list of what humans do when they behave intelligently. I remind myself that I am the adult, the one who should be displaying intelligence.

What Human Beings Do When They Behave Intelligently*

1. Listen to others.

Some psychologists believe that the ability to listen to another person, to empathize with, and to understand that person's point of view is one of the highest forms of intelligent behavior. (Oh, am I in trouble there!)

Parent note: You may put your hand over your mouth to accomplish this during especially traumatic discussions. Your teen probably will not notice.

2. Think flexibly.

Parent note: Parents of several teens have unlimited potential for dealing with several sources of information at the same time. Actually, flexibility is an absolute for survival. It helps if you thrive on the process and are not overeager for consensus of opinion.

3. Check for accuracy.

Reflect on the accuracy of information.

Parent note: "Hire a teenager—while he still knows everything!" When you are sure your teen has inaccurate information, hesitate, and then remember number 2 above as you decide how to communicate what you know.

4. Question and probe.

(Gently now, it's his music!) One of the distinguishing characteristics between humans and other forms of life is our inclination and ability to find problems to solve.

Parent note: This is not true if you parent teenagers. Problems that you aren't looking for are always finding you! What takes probing is finding enough solutions for all the problems.

5. Draw on past knowledge and apply it to new situations.

Parent note: I have informed my teens that I did not arrive at the church for my marriage in an ox-drawn covered wagon. My youngest asked that question as they were riding with me when I was driving an unfamiliar stick shift. I informed them that I learned to drive stick shift in a jeep in a cow pasture when I was twelve. Of course, then they wanted to know why they had to wait until they were fifteen to drive. (Answer: we don't have a cow pasture for them to practice in. Times have changed.)

6. Exhibit wonderment, inquisitiveness, curiosity, and enjoyment of the problem.

Intelligent humans are interested in diversity.

Parent note: Parenting a teen may expose you to more diversity than any other event in your life. I would never have been exposed to heat-sensitive shirts that change color where they touch the body, or to skate talk if I had no teens.

7. Exhibit ingenuity, originality, insightfulness, and creativity.

Parent note: Show me a parent whose kids are older than twenty-one—that person is an intelligent human being. He or she has my reverence and respect.

8. Use precise language and thought.

Parent note: Harry S Truman, not great by all measures, made an intelligent statement: "I have found the best way to give advice to your children is to find out what they want and then advise them to do it." That's precise thinking.

9. Realize that they are aware of their own thinking (metacognition).

This is the ability to describe the steps and sequences you are using before, during, and after

the act of problem solving. Intelligent human beings have the ability to analyze their thinking.

Parent note: When you are aware that you have lost your sanity, discontinue talking, if possible.

10. Decrease impulsiveness.

Intelligent human beings do not blurt out the first answer that comes to mind or make immediate judgments about an idea. Intelligent human beings read the directions.

Parent note: I think God forgot to put those directions in the diaper bag—especially when he sent my adopted kids.

11. Strategize and gather information before beginning a task.

Parent note: Oops, too late, teens are not returnable. On a serious note, the decrease in birth rate among some populations is not surprising when you consider the lack of support for parents and families.

12. Persist.

Intelligent humans persevere when the solution to a problem is not immediately apparent.

Parent note: One of my children once asked me, "Who won the human race?" Something tells me when my son is jogging from ages sixteen to twenty-one and I'm jogging from forty-five to fifty, he has a distinct advantage. My increasing wrinkles and gray hair testify to this fact. Just when a teen's hormones are in overdrive, his or her parents' hormones are saying, "Slow down."

13. Use all the senses.

See, taste, hear, smell, and feel.

Parent note: "Children need love, especially when they do not deserve it." That old saying is truer for teens and harder to live. "Dear Lord—my Jesus who has loved me at every moment of my life—help me to love, and love, and then love some more." Feelings can reach what intelligence cannot touch.

*Arthur L. Costa, *Developing Minds: A Resource Book for Teaching Thinking,* vol. 1, rev. ed. (Alexandria, Va.: Association for Supervision and Curriculum Development, 1991), 100-105.

What's a family for? Family is for learning to be We. Family is the first practice phase for living within guidelines. Family is for intervening and communicating. Family is for learning how to behave like intelligent human beings. Family is for persistent loving.

— 5 —
Different Worlds: The Male/Female Experience of Adolescence

One Day in the Lives of American Teens: 1990
  2,795 teens get pregnant
  1,106 teens have abortions
  372 teens miscarry
  1,295 teens give birth
  6 teens commit suicide
  7,742 teens become sexually active
  623 teens get syphilis or gonorrhea
  1,512 teens drop out of school
  14 teens die from drinking and driving

Vive la différence! Celebrate sexual diversity! This commentary on male/female sexuality has echoed for decades, perhaps centuries. Poetry (whether accurate or not) reflects how we view these differences.

Snakes and snails and puppydog tails,
that's what little boys are made of.

Sugar and spice and everything nice,
that's what little girls are made of.

By the time our youth reach adolescence, the presence of an X or Y chromosome at the moment of conception has significantly affected their lives.

Carrie experienced a different fear on prom night than was possible for Jeff. Ann, Carrie's acquaintance who had been sexually active for two years, experienced a sudden turn in her life's direction when she had an abortion. Ann's experience with her male partners, and the results of their sexual activity, was worlds apart from Carrie's.

Adults who work with kids see some stages where differences are not evident. As soccer enthusiasts watching our sons play, we noticed that some girls held their own on the field through age eight or nine. But then speed and aggressiveness differentiated their skills and success in mixed games. On the other hand, girls seem to develop verbal skills earlier. Size, hormones, and body composition begin to divide their worlds.

Boys and girls are undeniably different by adolescence. In addition to their differences, the presence of the opposite sex brings out a new personality. If you doubt this, observe a table of girls in a high-school cafeteria. Listen to them talk, hear the content of their conversation, and watch their body language. Then add an equal number of boys to the setting. Listen, hear, watch. A new female species emerges—created by the presence of boys!

Before you pronounce that boys are not affected by the presence of girls, picture teenage boys pigging out with no girls around. Now introduce into the scenario some young women they would like to impress. I predict that the volume of food they consume will decrease, and their manners will improve.

Different.

Adolescence finds our children grappling with new emotions in rapidly changing settings. And complicating their attempts at growing up is this confusing factor of being male—or being female. Sexuality in childhood had its influence. But here it becomes a propelling force.

Internally, hormones cause sweating, blushing, vocal changes, all at unexpected and inconvenient, if not embarrassing, moments. Externally, sexual awareness brings responses that are different. Hugs feel different. Looks communicate new messages. Reactions are different from the little boy/little girl world of comfort.

On the big journey of life, boy infants are put on one train track and girls on another. They run parallel courses for months and even years. But adolescence brings abrupt turns, taking them in increasingly separate directions. Some turns are important in the crises teens face. Some turns are unnecessary. Let's look at differences in female and male adolescents.

Vive la Différence—Maybe

Girls emerge from adolescence with a poor self-image, relatively low expectations from life and much less confidence in themselves and their abilities than boys. By the time girls are in high school, only 29 percent say they are happy with themselves, compared with 46 percent of the boys. High-school girls are much more likely than boys to say they're not "smart enough" or "good enough" for certain careers.

Students' interest in math and science starts out high in elementary school but drops as children get older. More girls than boys lose interest. Students who continue to like math and science through high school have much higher levels of self-confidence.

High-school girls are twice as likely as boys to perceive themselves as overweight. Pop culture tells boys not to worry too much about how they look because it's what they do that counts. Pop culture tells girls to worry about looks because for them all that counts is being beautiful and thin.

Forty-six percent of boys would tell if a friend were threatening suicide. Sixty-five percent of girls would tell.

In the classroom, males demand and receive more attention than females; boys call out answers to teachers' questions more often than girls by a ratio of eight to one. Males receive more praise, criticism, or remedial help; females get more neutral acceptance. Students who interact with teachers most are people who enjoy school and get better grades. Teachers' time and attention is the currency of the classroom. Boys are getting a bigger paycheck.

Forty percent of teenage girls experience pregnancy. This experience and the choices they make due to pregnancy are emotion-altering and life-altering experiences.

By the time teens take the Scholastic Aptitude Test, females on the average score fifty points below males on the math section and ten or twelve points lower on the verbal section, commonly considered females' strongest subject.

We can't celebrate all these differences. If we want to help teens in crisis, we need to look more closely at the observable turns on the female and male train tracks.

Sexual Activity

Statistics vary on teens' sexual activity. My objective is not to convince or to shock you, so you may choose any statistics you like. These statistics are people to me; kids, like the young father-to-be sitting in my office talking about the contract he had signed with the armed forces. His departure date is one week after the due date of his baby. Should he marry the girl he is quite fond of? Birth costs would be covered. He thinks he loves her.

During the same day, sitting in the same corner of my office, is a young mother-to-be. She is getting help through special education to cope with school, as is the eighteen-year-old father of her baby. She says "no way" would she marry Daryl now. "He's not ready to settle down." But she's planning to keep her baby. And she's fourteen.

Impact

Thirty-eight percent of all women and 9 percent of all men are victims of sexual abuse. The first instance of abuse usually occurs before age ten. Simply stated, before girls reach their teens, one-third have been initiated to sex in a negative, emotion-damaging way.

The next time you see a crowd of teenagers in

bleachers, a youth meeting, or a restaurant, think of the impact of that experience on those kids. A giant wall has been erected by an adult for one of every three girls and one in every ten boys. This wall will impact them in ways they cannot comprehend and sometimes may never overcome. These are the girls and boys, young men and young women who are more likely to engage in sexual activity early with their peers.

This spells *impact*. In a study of more than fifteen hundred boys and girls ages twelve through sixteen, 63 percent of the boys and 36 percent of the girls had had sexual intercourse at least once. Compared with virgins, nonvirgin girls were 2.5 times more likely to have used alcohol, 6.2 times more likely to have smoked marijuana, and 4.3 times more likely to have attempted suicide.

Boys engaging in premature sex were 2.8 times more likely to have used alcohol, 6.3 times more likely to have smoked marijuana, and 2.7 times more likely to have been arrested or picked up by the police than boys who had not engaged in early sex.*

*Dr. Donald P. Orr, "Premature Sexual Activities as an Indicator of Psychosocial Risk," *Journal of the American Academy of Pediatrics* 87 (February 1991): 141.

Another factor that spells *impact* is that most teens do not use birth control. Schools teach birth-control methods. Schools do a good job at teaching "plumbing"—the way the body works. But all this sex education is not affecting behavior. Complex attitudes and expectations are more powerful than information.

Girls often see agreeing to sex as a way to gain affirmation from their boyfriends. Because first sexual experiences are usually spontaneous, birth-control devices aren't available or utilized. Some girls feel that if they take precautions, the boy will think they were expecting sex and lose respect for them. If sexual contact isn't planned, the girls don't feel as guilty. Some girls believe that their boyfriends should be responsible for birth-control procedures, but most boys feel it is the girl's responsibility. With such disagreement, it is likely that neither will be protected.

Given these facts, the increase in teenage pregnancies is unavoidable. Before we talk about teen pregnancies, consider two other *impacts* of teen sexuality. Among high-school students who are sexually active, 14 to 18 percent of the girls in one study had chlamydia infections, as did 8 to 10 percent of the boys.

Chlamydia is a cross between a virus and a bacteria. The infection can cause scar tissue on the lining of the fallopian tubes, possibly blocking them. Infertility can be the result. Some experts report that in some locales, 40 percent of female teens have been infected. The syphilis rate for teenagers ages fifteen to nineteen has jumped 67 percent since 1985. More teenagers get the AIDS virus heterosexually than do adults. This happened despite the fact that condom use among teenagers doubled between 1979 and 1988.

Those of us who work with teens continue to be puzzled that health officials speak as though condoms promote safe sex. First, kids who know about them don't use them. Kids who use them don't use them properly. And for those who use condoms properly, there is an 18.4 percent failure rate.

According to a report published by the Alan Guttmacher Institute, 57 percent of American pregnancies are unplanned—and 47 percent of those pregnancies are to couples using contraception. Most of the latter pregnancies are due to improper contraceptive use, a common phenomenon among the young. (The Guttmacher Institute is the former research arm of Planned Parenthood.)

The increase in sexually transmitted diseases is more than a statistical phenomenon. A teenage girl sitting in a classroom and experiencing severe pelvic pain is afraid to tell anyone. She knows little about sexually transmitted diseases, just enough to be afraid.

An insidious piece of deception among teen girls is that sexual activity will make them feel better about themselves. The deception goes like this: you will feel mature, deeply loved, and bonded to your sex mate, and you will be knowledgeable and confident after you've "done it."

Not.

In one girl's words, "I felt used. I felt very pressured. The experience wasn't good. Two weeks later he broke up with me. I guess you could say it was the whole experience, not just the sexual part that was no good."

For this girl, and many others, a negative self-image fostered her belief that sexual activity is one way to be popular and hold on to boyfriends. By saying "yes," her self-esteem plummeted even further.

There is a high correlation between alcohol use and sexual experiences. Carrie's prom day is one example. An event that is supposed to make memories for a lifetime indeed does—the wrong kind. I have no statistics to document this, but I suspect the second most common incidence of first sexual intercourse (after incest) is in "celebrating" these special days.

In a close race for third place is date rape. We know that four in ten women experience rape. Some experts say it is 50 percent underreported. One study showed that rape increased four times faster than the country's overall crime rate over the last decade. Given the nature of adolescents—spontaneous, not thinking ahead, girls with low self-esteem, and 60 percent of our teens using alcohol regularly—the incidence of date rape has nowhere to go but up.

What surprises me is that people are surprised at the high incidence of date rape. Given the violence in the media (movies such as *Cape Fear,* which graphically depicts violence against women) and the lyrics of music that teens internalize as they listen, what do we expect?

I am sorry for the explicitness of what I write next. However, people who care about teens in crisis need to know what many teens are hearing. Lyrics in music depict sexual violence against women as fun.

"Me So Horny," a song performed by 2 Live Crew, describes how the male wants to break the girls' vaginal walls for his own satisfaction. He wants oral sex until she vomits. He wants to force intercourse in an abusive way until she is unable to walk. And then she is not to tell her parents, because her dad will be disgusted.

I feel strongly that parents should know exactly what music is saying to their teen sons and daughters and their peers. That is why I wanted to include six lines of the song, but Warner/Chappell Music denied me permission to quote them. They *did* grant a writer in *Newsweek* permission to reprint the lyrics because the article was promoting freedom of speech.

"Me So Horny" was popular when a New York jogger was nearly raped to death. The news report read like the song lyrics.

Lyrics of many songs may not be as bad; some are explicitly worse. Many movies are not as repulsive as *Cape Fear* but still communicate the same message. The connecting piece between these extremes and middle-of-the-road music and movies is this: Get power and use it for your own satisfaction. That theme promotes date rape.

I was reading an article about music groups that included some lyrics of popular songs. Realizing that many spoke of using women sexually, I asked my teenage sons if they were familiar with these groups and the lyrics of their music. My three sons were. I asked what their girlfriends thought of these songs.

While I don't consider my sons to be experts on girls' opinions, their answers may be pretty accurate on mainstream thinking. "The girls just like the music."

"Do they know what the words are saying?" I asked.

"They sing the words along with the music. They just don't pay any attention to what it means."

That may be all too true. They say the words and *internalize* the message without sending it through their mind and heart. The movies and music are protected by First Amendment rights of the artists, writers, and movie producers. But who will protect the girls' bodies?

I am not defending or excusing the sexual behavior

of our teens. What I am saying is this: What do we expect, given what we adults have permitted or promoted under the umbrella of free speech, individual rights, and power means right?

Pregnancy

Araselli sat in my office in baggy jeans, an oversized shirt, and her jean jacket. She clasped her hands tightly between her knees.

I began, "Some of your friends are concerned about you. They asked me to see if you're okay." I studied her emotionless face.

"What are they saying?" Her look was masked skepticism.

"Well, I can see that you've gained quite a few pounds. Are you feeling all right?"

Araselli launched into an explanation of her health, her most recent doctor visit, how she probably had an ulcer. The pieces of her explanation did not fit any rational pattern.

"What does your mom think about the weight you've gained?"

Her next explanation was about how she talked with her mother about everything. Our talk went nowhere. She had a secret. It appeared that she was even keeping it from herself. Denial.

Araselli gave birth to a tiny dark-eyed girl nine weeks before her graduation. Even after her daughter's birth, Araselli insisted she did not know she was pregnant until she went into labor. Her daughter's father is white; Araselli is Hispanic. Her mother protested to me on the phone that she never suspected that her daughter was pregnant and that Araselli could not bring that baby into her house. The mother had already raised her kids; she wasn't going to raise her grandkids. That was the morning after the baby was born.

Two weeks later Araselli was in the cafeteria with her friends clustered around her. Grandma was watching the baby. Three weeks later Araselli's mother not only had her granddaughter's room painted, she also was watching her during portions of every day so that her daughter could attend school.

The scenario is common: grandparents reentering the parenting role. Children having children and keeping them usually requires this. Parents protest, but they just can't bear to see their children struggle alone. Grandma may know exactly how it feels. One black woman described it this way: "When I became a mother at fifteen, I was angry. When I became a grandmother at thirty, I was d—d angry. But what could I do?"

Araselli's scenario is different in that she received her high-school diploma with her class on schedule. Most do not. Most teen mothers drop out of school. The crisis of pregnancy becomes a crisis of schooling and sometimes the determining factor for a lifetime career. Within the last two weeks, I have sat with single mothers in my office with their teenagers, one a male, and one a female, who were having difficulty academically. Both teens were not accountable in other areas of their lives as well. I listened as both mothers pleaded with their teens: "Don't blow it. Look how hard it's been for me. I couldn't graduate. I had you!"

My professional experience bears out the statistics that a teenage girl's crisis of pregnancy is somehow tied to the next generation's likelihood of repeating the cycle. In Araselli's case, her baby's father continued in school comparatively unaffected. The cycle is more likely repeated in females. Hopefully this will change with increasing emphasis and accountability for paternity and shared responsibility.

Teen Moms

It is a well-documented fact that more teen girls are deciding to give birth to their babies when they become pregnant. Keeping the baby is the norm rather than the exception. This varies with race, with black and Hispanic girls being most likely to keep their babies followed by white teens. In Illinois in 1988, 12.5 percent of all births were to teenage mothers. And 74.4 percent of the teenage mothers were unmarried.

One-eighth of pregnant teens in Illinois received no prenatal care at all, or not until their third trimester. This percentage is increasing rather than decreasing, though we have much more documentation on the importance of prenatal care, the increased incidence of low-birth-weight babies for teens, and the lifetime effect of this neglect.

Thirty-one percent of the teens aged fifteen to nineteen who gave birth in 1983 were having their second child, 24.4 percent were having their third, and 6.2 percent, their fourth baby. More than half of the $4,347,000 spent in fiscal year 1983 by the Illinois Department of Public Aid for medical expenses for births to teen mothers was for second and third babies. Pregnancy is the primary reason given by female students for dropping out of the Chicago schools.

Many resources and agencies are available to help pregnant teens and their families. In chapter 8, "Finding Help that Helps," I've listed specific resources with addresses. As a community and as citizens, we can all help.

What Can We Do?

As I look at statistics and listen in my office, I confess to a sense of helplessness and doom curling up the edges of my soul. However, I cannot let that feeling settle in and take root for two reasons. First, I believe in a God who is personally concerned about every person, teen girl and teen boy. I believe that God cares about his creation, especially his humans. Second, I care about kids. I work in a public school because kids matter—all shapes, types, races, and temperaments. These two beliefs convince me that we can still make a difference for some teen in some way.

The first step necessary is to face the facts. If you are reading this book, teens matter to you. Perhaps you have learned something about their world, some piece of information that compels you to take effective action. Accurate information is essential for helping teens in crisis. Accurate information about sexual activity and its consequences is a must if you want to be a difference-maker, a solution-finder.

Second, we need to take action on these facts. Unfortunately, I believe that the public in general has allowed special interest groups to dictate disastrous policy. We have accepted passing out condoms as a protection policy that has failed—and statistics prove it.

Special interest groups like Planned Parenthood are self-perpetuating. Their jobs depend on tax dollars for continued existence. To be on school property or near it, with a budget to spend on disseminating information, means they are employed doing something they believe in. But their activities and existence have not reduced the incidence of teenage pregnancy. And we, the general public, have not blown the whistle. We have let their lobbying power out-voice us to the detriment of our teens.

We have allowed the American Civil Liberties Union to promote freedom of speech over freedom of safety for the bodies of our young girls. I must tell you that I get quite upset hearing on the one hand the frequent protests about dissecting frogs for educational purposes, and on the other hand, the uncanny silence about rape.

Those of us who care about teens need to take courage and act on what we know. Some special interest groups are now well entrenched with lobbyists in the right places and well funded from sources like my teachers' union dues and the United Way. We need to take a deep breath, be courageous, and speak out in our living space—school, home, community, church, local political arena, and workplace.

Third, we need to rethink some "new" assumptions drawn in the last few decades. We know that males and females have been treated differently, often to the detriment of females. We made some attempts to correct this. Many are not working.

Women are created equal and therefore should have equal opportunity, equal pay for equal work, and a host of other equals. However, we have tried to equalize the male and female experience by treating boys and girls identically, ignoring some well-documented differences. We cannot equalize their experiences.

In our struggle to wipe out inequality, we pretend that vital differences are not there. Public schools are not permitted to accommodate these differences in educating children and teens. I think this increases the stress level on kids and the likelihood of crisis. Here are some differences we are not making room for:

- Girls speak and hear a language of connection and intimacy. Boys speak and hear a language of status and independence.
- Though given the opportunity to play together, usually boys and girls play in same-sex groups.
- Though some activities are similar, favorite games are different.
- Language used by girls and boys at play is different.
- Boys tend to play outside in large groups that are hierarchically structured. In their groups, the leader tells others what to do and how to do it.
- Boys boast of their skill and who is best at what.
- Girls play in small groups or in pairs.
- The center of a girl's social life is a best friend; intimacy is key.
- Girls' activities tend not to have winners and losers.
- Gender differences in ways of talking have been described by researchers observing children as young as three.

- Boys are encouraged to be openly competitive. Girls are encouraged to be openly cooperative.
- Girls seek to avoid conflict and preserve harmony. Boys may evoke conflict to improve their status in a hierarchy.*

*Deborah Tannen, *You Just Don't Understand: Women and Men in Conversation* (New York: Ballantine Books, 1990); Carol Gilligan, *In a Different Voice: Psychological Theory and Women's Development* (Cambridge, Mass.: Harvard University Press, 1982).

These complex attitudes are important and should not be ignored. Here's an example of how both sexes are disadvantaged when we try to equalize differences.

In our school, coed physical education classes are mandated by the state. I'm sure the objective is to support equality. It isn't working. Girls come into my office and tell me they are embarrassed in gym. Weight, whether they've shaved their legs, strength, clumsiness, and a myriad of other reasons make them feel embarrassed. What are they learning about physical conditioning in a mixed class where they perspire over their insecurities? Sometimes I'd like to say to our state headquarters, "You just don't get it. They are different."

My sons describe these differences in great detail when they explain why they prefer to be in the boys-only volleyball game in physical education. The competition and fun disappear immediately when the sexes are mixed, at least according to the boys in my home.

Vive la différence. After we've admitted and studied the differences of our kids, we need to let those facts dictate some differences in experience and settings for learning some topics. Variation is good. Different does not mean higher or lower, superior or inferior, powerful or weak. It simply means different.

Humans have a hard time letting differences be equal in value. We simply *have* to rank things and people. Humans *have* to flex their power. Only God-directed humans can say "different but equal." Different and respected. Different and esteemed. Different and preserved for those differences.

Helping teens in crisis will require God-directed intervention. Caring adults, armed with knowledge, need to examine the tracks that have been laid out for kids. We need to expose some deceptions and protect the freedom to live with male/female differences. We cannot ignore complex attitudes about power or historic expectations that our teens have internalized. Without intervention, increasing numbers of teens will be derailed.

We know that self-esteem influences behavior as sexual differences surface. Where do kids get their opinion of themselves? As parents or caring adults, can we make a difference? Let's explore the self-esteem factor.

— 6 —
Adolescent Self-Esteem: Oxymoron of the '90s

Should I include this chapter, I wondered? What's left to say? Any church or public library has at least a dozen books if not shelves on adolescent self-esteem. Now as I start to write, I question that I can condense what I want to say into one chapter! Three reasons have beaconed, whispered, prodded, and now *compel* me to write.

First, in our own family experience of teen crisis, we found no time or energy for library stops. (And perhaps a wall of shame would have kept me from entering a church library anyway.) If books were at our fingertips, we could not have read them in time when hospital trips, school communication, and sometimes law involvement, swirled through these times of crisis. These bounce in from one day to the next, one week to the next, and then ricochet for months when your teen is in crisis.

Sorting out what is helpful and accurate requires a clear mind, time, and emotional energy. When you want to help a teen in crisis, especially if it's your teen, you have none of the above.

> **Whatever the mind is bombarded with, the mind will accept.**

My second compelling reason is that of all that is in print on adolescent self-esteem, only a small part is really helpful to a parent with a teen in crisis. A bigger chunk may be helpful if you are a youth pastor, or educator, someone involved more theoretically with the problem and not living twenty-four hours a day with the person in crisis. The big chunk of information is good, but in reality, it is impossible to implement.

Parents read these books and feel guilty for all they wish they had done. Moms and dads who have expended every ounce of energy and have exhausted every intelligent idea they ever had, see their one weakness, the one time they blew it, and are pulled under by guilt. I know mothers who read self-esteem books about their kids and cry buckets. I don't know what fathers do.

Most books on adolescent self-esteem emphasize the early years. Studies repeatedly highlight mothers as if fathers don't exist. The early years are past; and Mom can't solve problems alone. So guilt and despair increase; courage and initiative shrivel like plucked wildflowers in the hot sun.

Let me illustrate.

Dorothy sat in my office. Her eyes were tired. Her once fitted jeans were now loose and faded. She needed a haircut and a rest.

"Thanks for coming in. How about coffee?" I knew she would say yes.

"Kim and Jimmy are struggling," I began. She nervously rotated the Styrofoam cup in her hand. "How are things at home?" I knew the divorce had been messy.

She started to speak. Something caught in her throat. Hopelessness, I suspect.

"I don't know what to do." Her voice was hoarse and quiet. "I switched to the day shift, so I'm home after school. But they're past me. Kim and Jimmy are more than I can handle."

Indeed they were. Her husband's gambling had gobbled the family income before the divorce. Alcohol and abuse forced her to leave her husband—an action she feared. Could she make it alone? She felt she had to try for her own safety and the safety of her children. As a nurse, she worked the night shift to earn more money. By the time she got home, running on black coffee but still exhausted, her teens should have been at school. Sometimes they were still sleeping; kids she didn't know were there, too.

The day shift meant less money and more fights with her kids. Her son started to gamble. When he lost money, he took out his frustration on his teenage sister.

"It sounds to me like you're doing the best you can," I said quietly. "How can I help?"

Floodgates opened. She just had to cry for a while before we could talk solutions. She wanted to help her kids through school. She wanted to help them feel better about themselves. But first she needed encouragement just to go on.

We expect too much of families today. Expectations for a family infrastructure that supports self-esteem was possible twenty years ago, given the typical family. Ten years ago, possibly, but not today. The world is different.

I asked a group of young couples what they wanted from family life. Their answers included the following:

- a haven from life's stress
- a place where they are accepted for who they are
- a place where they are loved unconditionally
- a comfortable place to live
- an attractive place to live
- children
- children who don't give them headaches
- a place to pursue their hobbies
- a place for recreation

I asked what they felt the family should provide for children; here are some of the answers:

- a place to grow and be healthy
- a place to learn
- a place to learn how to get along with people
- a place to learn to respect and obey authority
- a place to explore unique talents and abilities
- a place to develop healthy self-esteem
- a place to have fun
- a place to play

- a place to learn to work
- a place to learn accountability

I think we would all agree that children emerging from such a family untouched by the real world outside would enter adolescence with healthy self-esteem. After reading chapter 2, you know that the real world won't let that happen!

I believe that a few decades ago too much was expected of dads. Dad was to be the provider, energizer, spiritual leader, decision maker, disciplinarian, and on and on. Fortunately this imbalance was recognized, so many marriages now experience a more sharing relationship. Men and women are recognizing that a good marriage is the result of balanced whole people, not a Superman with the mate's self-esteem riding tandem.

We moved from the Superman era to the Superwoman era. Chapter 4 summarized what families look like today. Some Superwomen are raising families alone. Others are married with a full-time job outside the home and a full-time job inside—parenting. This era is extracting a terrible toll on women, families, and children.

The Superwomen era is fading into the Superfamily era. I see this decade as one where too much is expected of the family. Just as Superdad could not be all things to all family members, and Supermom cannot be all things to all people, the family cannot be all things to Mom, Dad, and each child.

What's a family for? We need to go back to a few basic simple things. Things like: (1) safety, (2) sanity, (3) survival skills, and (4) spiritual perspective. If family can accomplish these four, self-esteem will be a by-product.

When families try to do it all—and society expects more of the family than it can do—the family falls apart. Carrie's family was in the crumbling stage. Even basic functions were in jeopardy. If families can provide safety, sanity, survival skills, and spiritual perspective, I believe self-esteem will follow.

My third compelling reason for including this chapter is that the foundation for most self-esteem writing is wrong. Successful superficial recommendations based on the wrong foundation provide short-lived and superficial results.

Because of my profession, I read lots of material on building self-esteem in adolescents. The worldview writings collide head-on with Scripture. Speaking as a garden-variety philosopher and generic theologian (I may have just coined two oxymorons), these views cannot coexist. Our basic belief system is crucial. Current education-based philosophy on self-esteem stands in stark contrast to biblically based philosophy. *But they often look alike on the surface.* This deception is taking a big toll on adolescents *and* on parents and others trying to help them.

Because I am an in-the-trenches public high school counselor *and* a Christian, I would like to help you sort out what is accurate, good, and helpful, versus what is deceptive and destructive.

Self-Esteem's Only Foundation

Self-esteem in adolescents seems like a complex puzzle with many well-known pieces. Searching parents do well to learn how to encourage their children to discover and develop their abilities and strengths. But the most vital piece to the puzzle is often overlooked. That is the adolescent meeting, knowing, and accepting her or his Creator. Without that vital foundation, our adolescents today will not experience self-esteem.

Frank Peretti sums up the dilemma on his tape "God's Way or My Way" (available from Focus on the Family). I think his descriptions are quite accurate, and I would recommend that you and your teen listen to his entertaining and accurate account of the world's basis for self-esteem versus the biblical basis for self-esteem in adolescents. Let me describe our high-school students' dilemma:

We assign our impressionable freshman to Biology. The curriculum includes human development. We tell them they were once a blob of protoplasmic molecules. Then *POOF! POOF!* an accident happened. A cosmic intervention. This mass lurched, breathed, and heaved itself onto land. It mutated, survived, grew legs, grew a tail, ungrew a tail, leaned forward, stood upright, slapped its flattened forehead, and said, "I am human."

Next it evolved, self-selected, mutated, survived, slapped its forehead again, and said, "I've been a protoplasmic blob, an accident, a germ, an animal, and now I'm supposed to believe I'm somebody."

"Now class," the teacher says, "for tomorrow, know who Darwin is and the evolutionary theory." The bell rings. The God-created adolescents spill into the hallway bumping, laughing, thinking, feeling, wrestling with their lockers, shouting greetings, and hurrying to get to their Self-Esteem class on time.

"Now class," the self-esteem teacher begins, "turn to the page titled, 'Believing You're Somebody.' Our definition of self-esteem is on the board: 'Appreciating my own worth and importance and having the character to be accountable for myself and to act responsibly toward others.'"

It's obvious. Adolescent self-esteem is an oxymoron after teaching them evolution.

Author Stanley Coopersmith identifies four key components of self-esteem. He says that in order to have a positive self-image, people must feel:

1. Capable. Possessing skills and abilities.
2. *Significant.* Knowing that what they say, think, and do matters.
3. *Powerful.* Being able to influence the world around them.
4. *Worthy.* Believing they are unique human beings with special gifts, regardless of what they accomplish.*

*Stanley Coopersmith, *The Antecedents of Self-Esteem* (San Francisco: W. H. Freeman, 1967).

How can kids who are taught that they originated from nothing and that they exist now due to a series of accidents and mutations believe they are capable, significant, powerful, and worthy?

In the same semester, while they are learning the four elements of self-esteem, the media seduces them to believe that peer acceptance means having sex and looking appealing. They observe violence and may experience violence. How can they feel capable when it's tough to keep up in school? How can they feel significant when they are lost in the crowd? How can they feel powerful when they're scared? How can they feel worthy when they have been taught there is no right or wrong, no yardstick for measuring the value of truth or lies, good or bad?

Since there's no good or evil, there's no need for forgiveness or a Redeemer. It is a wonder that any adolescent has self-esteem considering what they've been taught about themselves!

I hope that real philosophers and theologians unmask this deception. I only know that as a Christian who reads Scripture with a believing heart, and then goes to work and sees the world of teens, hears what they are taught, feels the pull of media on them—it cannot work. There is no hope for teens to feel good about themselves apart from meeting their Creator.

Maybe a decade ago, the world was kind enough that superficial comfort could be found. No more.

Building on the Foundation

Once the foundation is in place, a teen, or any person, can develop self-esteem. Romans 12:3-5 summarizes the process: think accurately of yourself. From birth on, discover your strengths and weaknesses under your Creator's guiding hand.

The following list was made to help parents develop a sense of self-esteem in their young children.

• Tell your child that he or she is loved
  unconditionally.

- Talk and listen to your child often.
- Provide clear boundaries for acceptable behavior.
- Praise children often, and don't be afraid to praise in public.
- Find something positive to reinforce when a child's efforts have not been entirely successful.
- Offer children opportunities to make choices when possible.
- Work and play with children to help them develop their physical abilities.

The basis for each of these is biblical. No wonder they sound good! No wonder they work! These methods come easy to some parents. They experienced them in their own childhood; the role modeling feels familiar.

If you are a parent who did not learn these principles from your own childhood experience, they are hard to live. I understand. Though I did not experience them in my childhood, Jesus models them in how he cares for me.

Whether these happen in a parent/child relationship, significant other/child relationship, or Jesus/me relationship, three natural unmeasurables happen: connectedness, independence, and internal locus of control. A child goes into adolescence with a sense of belonging, confidence to make some decisions and take initiative, and an identity that comes from inside. She knows she is attached to special people called family, she can think through problems, and she's okay.

If you are a parent who has been successful living the seven methods on the previous page, you deserve applause, a rest, and assurance that your child will live securely ever after. However, self-esteem in all students drops through the school experience. The drop is greater in girls than boys, but both lose confidence.

I see at least two reasons for this. American schools pit student against student in competition: academically, athletically, artistically, and in every other category. And schools teach that boundaries are relative. Kids are in for brutal lessons in competition. Win the comparison battle at all costs. Jimmy had learned that his odds for winning were better at gambling than at academics.

Teens are also taught that they can make decisions as well as their elders and have a right to. This deception of world-based esteem versus biblical-based esteem denies the parent/child boundaries of Scripture. The worldview that there is no right or wrong, no good or evil, and that the child can decide erodes self-esteem. Current interpretation of the separation of church and state necessitates that clear boundaries be erased in our public schools.

We are reaping what we have sown in self-esteem.

A commonly agreed upon principle for self-esteem is that each person is unique and of value. But school only rewards certain qualities. Let me illustrate.

Last week I sat with my professional peers discussing a student who is unique. He is performing exceptionally well, considering his entrance test scores. Due to oxygen depravation at birth, his thinking is different, his looks are different, his gait is different, and his expression is different. He is disorganized, easily discouraged, and makes friends slowly. He needs daily medication to concentrate, and his appearance doesn't matter to him.

Recently this boy had a real self-esteem boost due to

his love of computers and ability to use a word processor. He likes to help others facing glitches.

I dug into an old file from a previous school for information on his learning. An unofficial yellow sticky note was attached that said, "Weird kid . . . etc. . . . etc." I confess to anger and a desire to identify the note writer and expose him or her to some of my garden-variety philosophies as well as a dose of generic theology! "Weird kid." *Not!* He is a human being created by God! Sin's existence in the world jumbled his genetic code, and unfortunate birth circumstances changed him for life. He is unique, needy, and valued by God. "Uniqueness" isn't valued anywhere, I fear, except in some families and in God's eyes.

Given the separation of church and state philosophy dictating schools' policies and the current climate in today's schools, self-esteem has nowhere to go but down in the school setting.

Dear parent, you are working against sizable odds to help build your adolescent's self-esteem. The greatest thing you can do is introduce your child to the Creator.

Teen Depression

When a teen is in crisis, it is unlikely that his helpers, caring people, parents, and others will *not* talk about his/her self-esteem. It is equally likely that the question will be raised as to whether the teen is depressed. Crisis shouts the question "Why?" Depression is a common answer and sometimes an accurate one. Sometimes crisis brings on depression. Sometimes depression brings crisis.

Teen Builders

- Value their uniqueness
- Focus on their strengths
- Treat people with equal respect
- Accept their feelings as valid for them at the moment
- Take them seriously
- Show faith and confidence in them
- Use "I" statements rather than "You" statements ("I'm frustrated when you're late. I wonder if you're okay.")
- Express your beliefs, values, and opinions as your own beliefs, values, and opinions ("I prefer earning and then spending.")
- Accept their beliefs, values, and opinions as theirs (at this time, anyway, they may be different forever or temporarily)
- Label behavior, not people
- Give constructive feedback: descriptive, specific, and immediate
- Establish appropriate behavior
- Establish logical consequences for inappropriate behavior
- Give choices when appropriate
- Model acceptable behavior
- Appreciate positive progress
- In problem situations, decide whose problem it is
- Focus on problem solving
- Build self-reliance
- Understand that everyone is responsible for his or her own feelings
- De-emphasize the importance of scores and winning
- Focus on participation, contribution, and satisfaction in activities and games
- Celebrate errors as a valid way of learning

Teen Bashers

- Use competition as a motivator
- Label the person, not the behavior
- Allow, promote, or model put-downs

- Expect your teen to voice your beliefs and values
- Give choices beyond his safety or competence zone
- Give your teen responsibility for your feelings
- Compare your teen with others
- Turn challenges into problems
- Set your teen up for criticism

To Do—Maybe

- Respect your teen's privacy.
  Yes, if his behavior is accountable. No, if there may be any illegal or safety issues (i.e., drugs, stealing, alcohol).
- Accept your teen's friends.
  Be as flexible and open as possible. You may draw the line if illegal, unsafe, or occult issues are involved.
- Open your home to your teen's friends.
  This is a team issue. Cooperatively set guidelines. Future invitations and parties depend on present guidelines being followed.

A fifteen-year-old girl may be reasonably happy, carefree, and accepting of herself. Date rape—one night's event, one experience, can cause depression. The severity, length of depression, and intensity will be affected by many factors following date rape; disclosure, support, medical attention, and a host of other things will determine the magnitude of the crisis.

Depression can also be genetically predisposed or environmentally induced, bringing a teen to a settled conclusion that he is worthless and should live no longer. He responds by attempting suicide. The crisis of a suicide attempt did not cause depression in this case. Depression was already an entrenched fact.

Determining the "why" of depression is complex in

most teens. Equally complex is deciding when a teen is clinically, diagnosably depressed. Tools like *Beck's Depression Inventory, Coopersmith's Self-Esteem Inventories,* and *Rosenberg's Self-Esteem Scale* help assess whether depression is a factor in your teen's crisis. In the chapter on finding help, we'll look at the medical criteria for diagnosis. Teens' normal downs may look like depression. The glands and circumstances of adolescents call for mood swings. Some teens dramatically show the world these ups and downs. It may be hard to call.

Just as depression will likely be considered in helping teens in crisis, the topic of suicide often surfaces. If the teen in crisis does not bring up the topic, caring adults should know that it has probably crossed his mind. A recent survey of eighth and tenth graders shows that one in three has seriously contemplated suicide. One in seven has attempted suicide. Every ninety minutes in the United States, a teenager is successful.

Since depression and thoughts of suicide may be part of a teen's experience in crisis, let's look at some warning signs.

Warning Signals of Depression
- Withdrawing from family life
- Spending most free time alone
- Socializing only with students much younger
- Using drugs or any suspected signs of drug use (medicating sad feelings)
- School grades dropping dramatically
- Behavior changing dramatically

As I talked with Dorothy about her daughter Kim, I mentally checked this list. All signals were on.

Warning Signals Related to Suicide
(signals listed above plus the following)

- Talking or writing about suicide or ending one's life
- Suddenly withdrawing from social contacts, interests, activities
- Loss of a loved one or even a pet recently
- Feeling like a failure; feelings of shame or guilt
- Referring frequently to death and dying; listening to mournful music
- Purchasing means of suicide, such as pills, rope, weapons
- Changing eating and sleeping patterns
- Changing behavior significantly
- Mutilating or abusing self, including alcohol/drugs
- Giving away one's personal possessions
- Lifting of sadness suddenly, or withdrawing (may mean that the decision to commit suicide has been made)

Kim had sent five of these signals. Her mom had not recognized the intensity of Kim's sense of loss, the severity of her depression. Being familiar with warning signals gave Dorothy an opportunity to intervene.

Unfortunately some myths persist that keep people from acting when their intervention is crucial. We talked about them. Dorothy was brave enough to talk about what she saw and face what she feared. Before Dorothy left my office, we had made an appointment for a free assessment of Kim at an adolescent trauma center. She knew and approved the program changes we were making for her daughter. She knew I was on her team.

Myths about Suicide

- Teens who talk about suicide seldom mean it.
- Alcohol is rarely related to suicide (90 percent involves alcohol).
- Most suicidal teens are severely mentally ill.
- Suicidal teens can be helped with lighthearted cheering up.
- Teens who talk about suicide are just looking for attention.
- Talking to teens about their suicidal feelings will give them the idea or cause them to attempt suicide.
- Depression is psychological and has little or no biological basis to it.
- A suicidal attempt is a typical, well-thought-out expression of an attempt to cope with serious personal problems.
- If someone wants to commit suicide, there is usually no way to prevent it.
- Teens who try suicide and do not succeed have gotten it out of their system and won't try again.

Facts about Suicide

- Individual at highest risk: white, male, over 65, retired or unemployed, single, ill
- Second highest: teens
- Suicide is in the top three leading causes of death for teens. Accidents and homicides are the other two. Some "accidents" may be in reality homicides or suicides.

- Nineteen cultures consider suicide an act of valor.
- For every boy who attempts, four to ten girls will attempt.

- For every girl who dies by suicide, four boys will die.
- Boys choose more violent methods for committing suicide.
- One suicide in a family removes the taboo for others.
- Eighty percent of persons who die by suicide have made at least one previous attempt.
- Cortisol, a hormone, measurable in blood tests, can help assess depression and stress related to suicide.

The Grief Connection

One common thread in adolescent as well as adult depression is the grief connection. Kim was grieving the loss of her dad as well as her dreams for an ideal family. Usually an unresolved loss underlies or precipitates feelings that cannot be denied.

While grief is intense emotional turmoil for all people, teens often grieve for reasons that adults don't understand and therefore ignore or deny. *Grief is a normal reaction to loss.* Teens' reasons include:

- Loss of a relative or friend through death, divorce, or relocation
- Loss of power or prestige
- Loss of body image
- Loss of security
- Loss of grade point average, scholarship, college entry
- Recognition that an important expectation is not possible
- Adoption losses (discussed in chapter 12)

Profile of Adolescent Suicide

Boy	Girl
Lost father before sixteen	Has domineering, self-centered mother
Father heavily involved outside the family	Has ineffectual father
	Looking for "love"
Spent some time away from home	Incidence of pregnancy predictably high

Both

Father seems to be central figure

Deep feelings of loneliness

Inadequate primary support group

Equate independence with the loss of parental love

Receive/send constant negative messages about self and life:

  "The world is better off without me."

  "I was meant to suffer and be a doormat."

  Can't accept a compliment

Since grief is in the perception of the one who is grieving, be careful never to label a loss "unimportant" or "trivial." You need not say anything or give advice. Just show that you care. Dorothy sat on the floor with Kim one night over a pizza and admitted that her family wasn't her dream either.

In our cluttered, busy lives, we want to hurry grief along. "Okay, it's over. Close the door. Walk away. Get on with life." But grief pays no attention to our time schedule.

The grief process normally lasts at least a year (longer with adoption), and repair does come with acceptance. Denial of the loss or minimizing it intensifies grief and can be an isolating experience. Kim later told me the "pizza talk" made a difference. "I don't feel so alone even when Mom's at work," she said.

Standing Together

As parents we are willing to guide our child through meeting his Creator. We do our best to help her discover strengths and weaknesses. Though these vital parts of developing adolescent esteem have their challenges, the greatest one is standing with our kids through crises. The best esteem builder is standing by them when you have good reason not to!

We cannot spare them the stuff of life that births depression and grief. We cannot prevent losses, disappointments, and tragedy in their lives. We cannot live through it for them.

I remember my young son grieving his bird's death. He lined his favorite lunch box with fabric, dug a grave under the most fragrant lilac bush, and handcrafted a memorial cross. I watched from the kitchen window, wishing his tears could be spared. All I could do was go and kneel beside him.

I have heard parents say, "Why couldn't it have been me?" or "Couldn't my child have been spared?"

If they faced no tough issues, if they made no wrong choices, if they never experienced a loss, they would never learn that you are connected to them beyond what is convenient. Parents seldom see the esteem this builds while teens are still teens. It's one of those long-term invisible investments. Jesus tells us he will never leave us. It's a promise that keeps us going; a promise we can mirror to our teens in crisis. Standing with them is an inner gift of esteem that people or time cannot take away.

━ 7 ━

School: From Struggle to Success

Have you ever felt that if your teen did not have to go to school, your life, as well as your teen's, would be much easier? I understand.

One Saturday morning, on waking Robb, he stammered, "You woke me from a bad dream!"

"What was your dream?" I asked.

"School."

Some adolescents love school, go willingly, cooperate with teachers and school rules, and at least attempt to do all the work assigned. This, however, does not describe all teens.

School is the biggest source of frustration in some parent/teen relationships. For these adolescents, going to school is usually a low priority, boring, and an unwelcome rite of passage to freedom and adulthood. Parents of these teens are dismayed at report cards and dread returning phone calls to teachers and attendance officers.

I have worked in public high schools for twelve years, so obviously, I am a believer in schools. However, schools are not the perfect environment for all adolescent learners. We do some things right. We do some things wrong.

When a teen is in crisis, it is unlikely that things are going well at school. Crisis eventually affects a teen's school experience in almost every instance.

Let's explore how you can become a three-way team—family, school, and student—so your teen can at least survive in the school setting. Success may be possible during the time of crisis. In fact, the school might offer a solution for the young person's unique needs. If the school cannot help or is creating the crisis, you need to know that fact so you can look for solutions elsewhere.

What Schools Can Do

"How can we keep our students from killing each other?" A city mayor making a presentation was asked this question recently in a forum for educators. Prior to his speech one student had killed two other students in the hallways of his school.

Most schools are not facing such drastic problems. Though your school is imperfect and cannot solve all teen problems, it may be able to help. Some resource or person may be part of the solution. Parent and school can work together on attendance, an appropriate program, and/or meeting special needs. Before analyzing each of those three areas, let's look at a vital key to *any* solution, including the school, whether it be attendance, programs, or special needs.

Home/School Communication

I am convinced that parents cannot be a positive part of their child's school experience—whether the child is five or eighteen—unless there is two-way communication. Likewise, the school cannot succeed unless it links to a student's family. I wish I could tell you that the school will contact you as soon as they see any problem. This is unlikely today even in the most highly rated schools in our nation.

I see communication between school and home deteriorating at a hazardous speed. The *need* for communication is escalating at an equally fast pace. Most schools have prescribed mailings to parents: report cards, progress reports, and a limited number of informative pieces. Beyond this, the school will not initiate contacts with parents for the majority of its students.

Dear parent, as tired and frustrated as you are, you will likely need to be the initiator and persistent communicator in order to get help from the school. Here are some suggestions.

Attendance

If your teen is in crisis, whether over a temporary circumstance or a severe, entrenched problem, he or she may prefer to avoid school, or at least some classes. School systems rarely report class absences to parents within twenty-four hours. Often school policy is that parents are notified after three cuts. I registered a student transferring from a school where he had not attended class for two months and the parent had not been notified. If you are unsure about your school's policy on reporting, ask.

With probably one phone call, you can determine who to contact to check attendance. The school policy for reporting attendance may or may not be working for your teen. Some kids beat the system—even a good one. Some systems don't work. In that case, you may as well know this quickly so you can look for help from other sources. You will want to know whether your teen is in school, and whether he or she is in class when in school.

School Records

Based on the Family Educational Rights and Privacy Act (the Buckley Amendment, 1974)

1. All parents, even those not having custody of their children, have access to each education record that a school district keeps on a child.

2. School district must obtain parent's permission in writing before disclosing any personally identifiable record on a child to individuals other than professional personnel employed in the district and certain other persons.

3. Right to challenge contents of records through a hearing in order to correct/delete any inaccurate, misleading, or otherwise inappropriate data and to insert written explanation of content

---

If the policy is loose, enlist the help of the principal and ask that you be notified after one cut or one absence. If your teen is cutting classes or school entirely, your knowledge of this is not the equivalent of a solution. But at least it will help you see the big picture. If school truancy is an important part of the crisis, and the school's system is ineffective in finding solutions, you may need to consider another school placement. We'll talk about that in the next chapter. Meanwhile, you as a parent need to know whether your teen is in school.

Programs

Attending school does not guarantee accumulating credits and a diploma. All schools have student report cards, but not all parents see them. Communication can fall apart at any point. I talked to one parent who had not seen a report card for an entire school year. Kids often get to the mailbox before parents do.

Most schools have midterm reports that are either mailed or sent home with the student. If you aren't getting anything from the school, call. Get in touch with a counselor, a teacher, the principal, even a custodian or a secretary. Contact someone and find out how to get information.

Many parents have horror stories about school communication. I have a few with my own children. But in most schools, if you ask long enough, and enough people, eventually you will get answers. They may not be the ones you'd like to hear. But you need to have answers in order to make decisions about schooling.

What does a report card report? Many parents are confused about this. A report card does *not* tell you how intelligent your student is, or whether your student is learning. The report card just tells you whether your child is "doing school."

Some kids "do school." Some kids do not. I believe all parents know whether their kids do school. We can feel it. A report card shows it, but a parent feels it with or without seeing a report card.

"Doing school" means that the student meets the teachers' expectations in the classroom. Kids who meet the teachers' expectations get good grades. Doing school means they follow the rules well enough to avoid negative consequences. Following the rules means that parents don't get mailings about failure, or phone messages assigning detentions, etc.

"Doing school" also means that the school is offering a program that is effective, *given who the student is*. The "goodness of fit" principle applies to kids/school in the same way as child/parent. "Fit" is complex. For example, we know that many inner-city schools are inefficient and lack discipline and control. Students get lost in the inertia and drop out. One of Chicago's schools loses 75 percent, a clear call that students aren't "doing school!"

In these same city schools, however, Indo-Chinese refugee children "do school." They are a minority population, living in crowded conditions, sitting in the same classrooms, and succeeding. Why are they successful? Because they spend an average of three hours and ten minutes on homework a night and are expected to help younger siblings at home. Parents read aloud, often in their native language. The family expectation fosters interdependence and family-based orientation, not independence and individual achievement. Families do not emphasize fun and excitement as objectives. Asian families feel shame to be on welfare. They do not expect school to be a social-service provider. They expect an education. Thus, the "fit" between kids and school varies with ethnic background.

I said earlier that doing school means the school is offering a program that is effective *given who the student is*. Your friend's teen may be successful in a program where your teen struggles. From our chapter on knowing your teen, we know that students are different.

Learning styles affect which students do school. People with common sense have always known this. School lays out a red carpet for the organized, right-brain, logical student to love being there. Not so for the creative, imaginative, left-brain daydreamer. This has nothing to do with intelligence. Remember, Einstein failed math. He didn't do school.

Your teen's crisis may be heightened or even caused by a mismatch between his or her school program and his or her learning style.

So what makes an effective program? Our only conclusion is that an effective program for any student means a fit between the student and school. This fit includes motivation, readiness to learn, and some factor of ability. You may be able to help your teen in crisis by examining and talking about these factors.

If school work is sagging, by all means, ask why. Armed with those answers, get the other side of the story.

Ask what would motivate your teen to do better at school. You may have to impose your own rewards and restrictions to make it through a demotivated time.

The "readiness to learn" factor is often determined by the stuff in a young person's life. If a divorce is pending, date rape has occurred, or a move is imminent, without a strong support system the student is unlikely to enter a classroom focusing on the subject at hand.

Another factor to be explored is whether your child can learn by the method used in his school and classroom. Usually students with learning difficulties have been identified by the time they're ready for high school if they have attended an accountable grammar school. But that's not always the case. You can ask for evaluations of learning, speech, hearing, and sometimes psychological disorders. A disability may not have surfaced. Or a student may have been bright enough, persistent enough, or have enough coping and accommodating skills to get by—until high school. Or until a crisis comes. I have seen this increasingly in my years in education. When schools were less burdened with endless expectations, families were more stable, and society provided a more supportive environment, more kids could do school.

With schools becoming less nurturing and less safe and secure, some students who might have made it through simply cannot make it anymore. Special education programs help many of these students.

Briefly summarizing, the special education program policy states that no person can be deprived of an education due to a handicapping condition. The handicapping condition may be obvious in the case of hearing loss or blindness. It may not be so obvious for a learning disability, attention deficit disorder, or mild fetal alcohol syndrome.

In reality, with reduced funding for schools today,

special education programs may be a carrot dangled before parents and students that does not, in fact, exist.

Investigate what programs your district provides and ask how students can gain access to them. You can request a student evaluation. Typically these programs offer more structure, smaller class sizes, an aide to the teacher, and flexibility in scheduling. If your teen is not making it in the regular school setting, check these out.

Criteria for Special Education

The Education for All Handicapped Children Act (P.L. 94-142, 1975) is an enforceable civil rights act for exceptional children. The major features are:

1. That all handicapped children be provided access to a free, nonarbitrarily determined education and related services

2. That these programs and related services be designed to meet the unique needs of the child

3. That all handicapped children be educated in the least restrictive environment

4. That an individualized educational program be designed for each child

5. That all children covered under the law and their parents were entitled to procedural due process protections.*

*H. C. Hudgins and Richard S. Vacca, *Law and Education: Contemporary Issues and Court Decisions,* 2d ed. (Charlottesville, Va.: The Michie Co., 1985), 402-403.

Special education may work due to the structure and small class size. As a parent, you may decide to choose these benefits through a private school rather than public school special education. We'll look at some of those options in the next chapter.

Special Needs

Terry's parents sat in my office exuding frustration. "What's his problem? He's failing classes and blowing his chance for a football scholarship. He's not dumb!"

Factors that interfere with a good fit between a student and school vary from physical to cultural and emotional. I've included a list of characteristics on underachievers and another list of the characteristics of attention deficit disorder. These lists are not perfect diagnoses, but if a characteristic seems probable, talk to resource people, look in the library, and investigate more thoroughly to find workable answers. These lists may help you recognize and identify your teen's need.

Terry's parents compared this information with what Terry was doing at school. They answered their own question.

Reasons Kids Underachieve

- *Inability to express anger directly.* Anger is expressed indirectly by withholding school performance and thereby "punishing" parents.
- *Fears of growing up.* Some kids want school to last forever in order to avoid responsibility.
- *Fear of success/feelings of inadequacy.* Some kids fear success because expectations will rise. They may find it difficult to separate from their families of origin.
- *Anxiety.* Success is an all-or-none phenomenon. Getting a 99 instead of 100 feels like failure. They have trouble finishing tasks and are often inattentive and confused.

- *Low self-esteem.* This may be triggered by atypical life experiences (such as parental divorce, being adopted, moving frequently, and having to constantly change schools and make new friends). A vicious cycle is created: avoiding schoolwork because of fear of criticism brings failure, which lowers self-esteem.
- *Depression/emotional problems.* A drop in school performance can be a cry for help. A sudden drop in grades can be an indication of substance abuse, sexual abuse, or other emotional trauma.
- *Self-fulfilling prophecy.* If the underachievement goes on for a long enough period of time, it becomes a part of the person's self-concept.

Terry matched the first four characteristics. His parents decided they needed to talk with him about more than his most recent successful football plays. Since they described him as easily distracted, we looked at another possibility.

Characteristics of Attention Deficit Disorder

1. A disturbance lasting at least six months during which at least eight of the following are present:
    - often fidgets with hands or feet, or squirms in seat (teens may be limited to subjective feelings of restlessness)
    - has difficulty remaining seated when required to do so
    - is easily distracted by extraneous stimuli

- has difficulty awaiting turn in games or group events
- often blurts out answers to questions before they have been completed
- has difficulty following through on instructions from others, not due to oppositional behavior or failure of comprehension (for example, fails to finish chores)
- has difficulty sustaining attention in tasks or play activities
- often shifts from one uncompleted activity to another
- has difficulty playing quietly
- often talks excessively
- often interrupts or intrudes on others (for example, butts into other children's games)
- does not seem to listen to what is being said
- often loses things necessary for tasks or activities at school or at home (toys, pencils, books, assignments, etc.)
- often engages in physically dangerous activities without considering possible consequences, not for the purpose of thrill-seeking (for example, runs into the street without looking)

2. Onset before the age of seven
3. Does not meet the criteria for a pervasive developmental disorder.*

*Robert L. Spitzer, M.D., *Diagnostic and Statistical Manual of Mental Disorders,* 3d ed., rev. (Washington, D.C.: American Psychiatric Association, 1987), 52-53.

Terry's parents recognized that Terry did not meet the diagnostic criteria for ADD; however, the characteristics of underachievement gave them insight into their son. Academics did not come easily. Athletics did. As much as he loved high-school football, he feared the demands of college competition, including the classroom. The more his parents pushed, the quieter and angrier he became.

Psychological/Emotional Effects of ADD in the Classroom
- Lack of confidence due to lack of success
- Anxiety—tries hard, still fails, becomes more anxious
- Low self-esteem
- Depression—feels helpless and hopeless
- Sensitivity—becomes overly sensitive, then defensive
- Defense mechanisms—projects blame to protect self-esteem

Possible Results of ADD by Adolescence
- Academic shutdown ("I can't; and I don't care.")
- General feeling of inferiority ("I'm nothing.")
- Defensiveness—depression/aggression ("Teachers don't like me.")

Armed with more information, parents can make better decisions for success. One step may be recognizing that your dream for your teen's school experience is impossible. Success, in many parents' memory, is a letter jacket or band sweater and a traditional diploma. Success today for some achieving young adults I know is:

- a diploma earned from a correspondence school at age twenty-one, and two years of apprenticeship training in construction

- a Graduate Equivalent Degree issued at age nineteen and a healthy baby in her new adoptive home, with biological mom considering junior college
- a home-school diploma earned at an individualized pace with a healing body from a diabetes crisis

For Terry, it was telling his parents he wanted to try a junior college with intramural football first. Their permission freed him to bring his grades back to passing. He no longer feared graduating.

One positive about our changing times is that alternatives for earning a diploma are mushrooming. We'll talk more about these in the next chapter. Dear parent, giving up your dream for your teen's high-school experience is not failure. It is a required step of success in light of the facts many teens and their parents must face.

My son, Charles, reminded me last night that parents shouldn't feel guilty about their kids' problems; it's not their fault.

"It's nasty out there!" were his exact words.

Success, by my new definition, is standing with your teen and making a good decision for the future based on what's real today.

— 8 —
Finding Help that Helps

The phone rings. A sixth sense stirs something behind your consciousness; your insides know what your mind refuses to think; your heart tries to turn over and gets caught sideways.

"This is Sergeant Reynolds from the juvenile division. We have your son."

Failure is an event, not a person.

You think that you are the only parent who lies awake through the night, rising from your crumpled pillow with every passing set of headlights that illuminates your driveway.

You envy families whose teenagers are asleep in their homes. You wonder where your troubled child/adult is. Is he sober? Is he speeding on some strange dark highway, alert enough to stay on the road? Is he alone? Is someone forcing him to places he would never go and experience things he would never try if he could choose? Your mind travels to new imaginations, backtracks, retraces, thinks in circles, refuses reason and sleep.

Through the shadows you search the space where your mate's familiar form usually lies. Empty. A dim light filters from the hallway. You shuffle with furry eyeballs to the kitchen. He sits slightly slumped toward his coffee cup. Head in his hands. Shoulders stooped. He succumbs for the moment to the fears that neither of you have spoken. You have walked through so much together. But somehow there seems to be no "through" this time.

No "Exit."

No "The End."

No "Reprieve."

Your small, tousled, curly-headed child could at one time be placed in a playpen for safety and given a toy to soothe dissatisfaction. But things have changed.

Yes, things have changed.

Problems facing adolescents are different.

Families are different.

Our world has changed. Some resources our parents and grandparents had are no longer available (like extended families and a simple life-style). Though we will talk about many possible solutions and resources in this chapter, first I would like to communicate two messages to parents: you are not alone, and you should not assume all the blame.

Before we share options, I would like to encourage you, offer you comfort, a hug if it were possible, and my empathy for you in crisis.

You Are Not Alone

You feel alone. But when you can share what you are experiencing, you will discover that you are not alone. Other families struggle. There are support groups and compassionate people who will walk with you. No one has walked precisely in your footsteps, lived with your teen, experienced crisis exactly as you have. But many *have* lived through similar events and felt similar feelings.

We gained immeasurable strength from these parents. We collected understanding hugs and felt literally nurtured in their presence. Some parent somewhere does understand some of your crisis and feelings. As you discover these people, your feelings of loneliness get pushed back to make room for new networks and friends.

Do Not Assume All the Blame

When our child/adult is troubled, we are painfully sensitized to every parenting mistake we ever made. But blame is a heavy cloak. And whether we put it on ourselves or someone else flings it on our shoulders, it drags us down, resolving nothing.

I hope that from reading the earlier chapters on what the world is like for teens, genetic differences, and increasing changes and pressures on families, you recognize that you are not the only influence or power in your teen's life. May I graciously and kindly state: you are not that important.

In fact, to help your teen, you have to leave self-blaming and pity-partying behind, or you will be the problem rather than the solution.

Teens in crisis need more than parents. Let's look at some helpful resources.

Discovering Who Can Help

You may naturally ask when your teen is in crisis, "Who can help us?" Good answers are discovered by asking that question with an open mind. One frequently considered solution is extended family. Mentally you check off: grandparents, ex-spouse (this resource is frequently tried), aunts, uncles, etc. "If my teen were living with someone else, in a different environment, would the crisis pass? Would things get better?"

However, a second question is vital. "What events are happening in my teen's life?" New people in a person's life will not necessarily solve problems or change events.

Finding different people to help may be a good solution if goodness of fit is the main source of crisis and conflicts for a teen and his or her family. But a change in who your teen is living with is not a good solution if there is substance abuse, addiction, or school failure. In that case, the event (use of substance or school failure) must be addressed.

I suggest that you make two lists: a "who can help" list, and a "what's happening" list. The "who" list should include the resources that come to your mind of people or organizations that can help you. The "what" list should include the events and behaviors in your teen's life that are creating the crisis.

Your lists might look like these:

Who Can Help

Uncle and/or aunt
Grandparent(s)
Ex-spouse
School (public or private)
Church
Parachurch organization
Shelter or alternative for home
Hospital
Counseling
Self-help group

What's Happening

Failing grades
Mood swings: pervasive sadness or hysteria
Truancy
Breaking school rules
Precipitating family arguments and fireworks
Poor "fit" with family members
Making poor decisions
Underachievement
Violence to others
Violence to self
Running away
Abusing drugs or alcohol
Refusing to follow appropriate guidelines

Every parent's list is different. Even though it may be difficult to sit down and calmly make these lists, they may spare you looking for solutions that won't work.

If your teen's problem is not yet a crisis, some options are helpful that will lose their impact when the crisis escalates. For example, a teen who is making poor decisions may respond to counseling and need no other help. A poor fit in a family can be addressed successfully by family counseling if it is started before members have given up or abuse has occurred. Counseling alone, however, may not be enough when there is violence and addiction.

Counseling can successfully perform four functions: (1) giving information, (2) helping the person get in touch with feelings (psychotherapeutic), (3) training in parenting, and (4) training in decision making. It's certainly worth looking for this resource when your teen is struggling or in crisis. Three different systems help teens in crisis: the educational system, the medical system, and the juvenile justice system. If counseling doesn't offer enough help, check out these three systems to see what is available and appropriate.

If the problem seems focused at school, you'll want to look for help there. As we covered in chapter 7, special education may help with learning or behavioral difficulties. If the school cannot help, you need that information so you can look elsewhere.

Extended Family

Families often send their distressed teen to another relative or ex-spouse (in case of divorce). From my position as a counselor in a high school, I see that this solution doesn't work very well in these cases:

- substance or alcohol abuse
- conflict between the parent and the person assuming custodial care
- entrenched emotional and/or behavioral problems
- lack of effective means of control of the teen by the new caretakers

I have registered new students with the new custodial parent, studied a checkered transcript scattered with *F*s and a poor attendance record, and watched the teen continue old patterns in a new setting. I have watched new students get connected with natives who have the same habits that the student's parents were hoping he'd escape. This is not *always* the case. But it's true so often that I want to warn parents. Sometimes what they think is a new start is a false start and must be repeated in a new setting that can potentially address the student's problem.

Henry Ford once said, "Failure is the opportunity to begin again more intelligently." I feel bad for parents who think they have a solution and then have to begin again. Getting more information up front might help you avoid a false start. New people in a young person's life will be a successful solution *only if the teen can respond and change his or her behavior in the new environment.* Asking these questions might help you determine whether moving your son or daughter to a new location is a good decision:

- Does the new caretaker have the resources to address your teen's problem in at least three areas: emotional, educational, supervisory?
- Assuming you are not relinquishing legal custody, can you communicate and cooperate together for the good of your teen?
- Is your teen willing to try in this new environment? (Some resources are effective even if he or she is unwilling, but extended family solutions require *some* cooperation by the teen.)

School Choices

If you have discovered that your public school cannot help you, there are other options. Before throwing up your hands in despair, consider private schooling or home schooling. Some parents quickly say, "I can't afford it!" or "Impossible!" I cannot promise you that either is a good option for you *or* that either will work. But I am saddened to see parents draw that conclusion before getting good information. Often parents have options they haven't discovered.

Just as necessity is the mother of invention, desperation is the mother of innovation.

Private schools come in many sizes, shapes, and colors. Since communities have great variety, let me suggest how to search and compare options.

Talk to individuals you know who are using other options. They can tell you what they like about their choice of private school and what they know they are giving up by choosing that option.

Scanning our community, we saw that private

schools fell broadly into two categories: religious and special needs. All had smaller classes than public schools, thought by many parents to be one of the greatest benefits. The costs for religious schools in our area were similar among nonboarding schools: both Catholic and Protestant were approximately $150 per month with some additional fees. Alternative schools specializing in students with special needs were approximately $350 per month.

The special needs served ranged from giftedness to mild learning and behavioral difficulties. Some academies promised college preparedness and high college entrance test scores. And some of them deliver. Many pretest to be sure they are admitting kids who have the potential to benefit from what they offer. Any credible school should give parents the names of families who have used their services so they can give you firsthand information.

None of the schools in our area had their own buses, but some districts provide busing to parochial schools. Transportation is a neutral service not promoting religion and thereby upheld in the courts as a fair use of local tax dollars.

Home schooling has long been the educational method of choice for parents who oppose the teachings and atmosphere of public schools. I see this as an option that parents may increasingly use as schools become less able to meet specific challenges of teens. School environments often present poor options for students. Condom distribution and abortion advocacy added to theories of evolution and amoral values simply are unpalatable to many families. As the disadvantages of public schools increase, home schooling will look better to some families and can be used for a temporary period.

American School is a correspondence school in Chicago, Illinois. Students can utilize this school to make up credits or compensate for a semester of crisis. Many public schools will accept up to two credits (the equivalent of a semester) toward the diploma. A one-credit class costs approximately $150.

ACE is a Christian correspondence program that can be used in the home as well as in alternative housing options. Many publishers and Christian colleges and high schools offer correspondence classes. Some parents and teens choose their entire high-school option from these; others, a semester or a few credits.

One Christian high school in our area provides home-schooling texts, workbooks, and scoring of tests, and issues a diploma for $280 per school year.

Individualized tutoring can help some teens with their academics during times of crisis. Hourly tutoring rates may vary from $10 to $40 and are often a good investment to help kids earn credit while struggling with academic deficiencies or other problems.

Military academies have been an option since our country was founded. Most provide boarding and non-boarding options. The costs for boarding are approximately $1,500 per month. Some have scholarships or other sources to help reduce that cost. Midwest area academies are primarily for boys. One benefit of these schools is structure and learning to respect authority.

Dear parent, let me digress a moment. If you are reading this thinking, "I can't," consider the consequences of trying nothing. I'm an educator, so obviously I value education. Your teen *may* reap some lifetime benefits from your attempt to try another schooling method. Private, nonboarding costs may equal your payment on a new television or a good sound system, items that will be obsolete or broken before your teen is twenty-five.

Someone has said, "If you always do what you've always done, you'll always get what you've always got." Trying a different school setting may be an effective intervention. Diverting dollars in your personal budget, or scraping, scrounging, and sacrificing may bring a new solution. If not, then you can say, "I did the best I could."

Church and Parachurch Organizations

Some churches offer an elaborate menu of assistance; some, a cup of cold water, and others, nothing. Some churches consider adolescent crisis a "family only" issue, and others are an effective part of the team.

Many offer counseling or make referrals to community sources. Some have affiliate schools or alternative homes. These may be miles away, which can be an advantage. I encourage parents, after seeing what their church offers, to evaluate whether this addresses their teen's particular problem.

Some church or parachurch organizations require teen willingness; others do not. For example, Freedom Village in New York requires willing students. It is in an agricultural setting and schooling is through ACE (correspondence based, individualized). The cost is $650 per month.

New Horizons in Indiana will take unwilling students. They have several homes. The one in the Dominican Republic has been helpful to teens using drugs or alcohol. New Horizons is highly structured, and students must earn rights.

Some options are more like camps, take only a few teens at a time, and are more of a nurturing, foster-family environment. Academics are often secondary in these settings. Don't rule them off your list because of that; some teens need turning around before they can focus again on their studies.

Large parachurch organizations such as Focus on the Family have lists of resources for teens. Usually they do not endorse specific institutions, but they are willing to give information—addresses and phone numbers for parents to pursue.

The options for pregnant teens vary from staying home and continuing schooling (public schools can no longer exclude them, though they may provide alternative facilities), to choosing a different setting. In our area, crisis pregnancy centers can serve most girls by providing a home until the baby is born and then assist with adoption placement if that option is chosen. Well-known organizations such as the Salvation Army and Evangelical Child and Family Services also assist pregnant teens. They help with health benefits and provide information for decision making, whether single parenting, marriage, or adoption is chosen.

Shelters and Alternative Homes

Most communities have shelters for children and/or teens in crisis. Typically these are short-term, and a child or teen can go to them for temporary safety or to get off the street if they've run away and are afraid to go home. Shelters may have a four-week limit during which another place must be found, either by the family or the court.

When a teen arrives at our local shelter, a caseworker immediately begins networking to find a safe and work-able home. Custodial parents are always the first choice. If this is not possible, extended family is the second option. Awarding the child to the state is the last.

Many states have a provision for sheltering teens who are out of control. In Illinois, a petition may be filed in court called "minor requiring authoritative intervention." A parent can ask the local law enforcement agency for this assistance if the teen is endangering others, re-peatedly disregarding curfew, or running away. Most law enforcement agencies hesitate to enforce it or even make its availability known. (Maybe they fear that frustrated, tired parents will deposit busloads of teens in their pre-cinct offices! Some readers may not appreciate my hu-mor; others of you know the feeling exactly. When we're not crying, we might as well laugh!)

Hospitals

Since hospitalization is an increasingly popular option, I am including an entire chapter on making that choice and surviving as a family through and after the hospitaliza-tion. This may be the only option if medical problems or safety from suicide are involved. If you are considering this option, call your insurance provider and ask for specific information on coverage as well as which facilities meet their criteria.

Counseling

Counseling is a logical first step when parents see teens struggling and making poor decisions. The four functions of counseling listed earlier may come from likely, structured resources or unlikely, surprising ones. I have a strong bias for seeking Christian-based counselors and would recommend contacting local church and parachurch organizations for referrals.

Sometimes community services or youth organizations help. I have seen caring people who did not consider themselves counselors help teens get in touch with their feelings and sort through options. Our son had two youth leaders who were like midwives. They helped birth his faith from family umbilical cord to his own conviction that he would live for the God who created him.

I have seen parents training other parents by their example. Mentors are often sources of good counsel.

Christian clinics seem to be sprouting all over. They offer individual counseling and group sessions as well as hospital referrals. Since fees vary greatly, I'm not including numbers. If cost seems prohibitive, ask if the organization has a sliding scale based on need. Many do, which may reduce cost by one-third.

Self-Help Groups

Since the inception of groups such as Alcoholics Anonymous, many adults have gained encouragement and strength from the power of the group. Though self-help groups for teens are not as common, some are available in some areas and encourage or give information for the family.

Directory of Self Help & Mutual Aid Groups* lists hundreds of self-help groups and gives phone numbers and addresses to get more information.

*Directory of Self-Help and Mutual Aid Groups, 7th ed. (Evanston, Ill.: Self-Help Center)

I have seen adolescents in crisis get help through groups like Al-Anon and groups for adopted teens. Though most teens are not eager to walk into a group of strangers, many are willing when they know the group will address a common need.

Group support for parents can be a real plus. Local churches are waking up to this crying need in their neighborhoods. Many parents whose teens are in crisis know caring people in their church. But these caring people don't know how to help them. Problem-specific groups can. For example, if your teen has Attention Deficit Disorder, you will learn coping skills and parenting skills and get excellent references for medical support by attending a parent group for ADD parents.

Groups for parents who have lost a child through death give comfort and understanding that others simply cannot offer. In addition to the self-help book I mentioned above, local Yellow Pages list resources. Churches, schools, or community services may have information. Usually local newspapers devote a section to group meetings, times, and locations.

You may benefit from a group temporarily or for

years. Many are flexible, people come and go, but the structure is there when you need it for leaning or getting information.

My husband and I talked to dozens of people when we were searching for help. Probably a hundred people knew about some part of our need. Our coffee-stained notes of addresses and phone numbers, smudged yellow stickys of names and resources, and crumpled pamphlets became a file we returned to, after they had served us, to help others. One friend had Searched (capital *S* intended), updated, and typed his resources to share with us when we called him for help.

We recently met him and his wife for spinach-stuffed pizza to catch up on our kids.

"You guys are lucky," Frank said. "When we needed help, there were no lists of resources. Even national parachurch organizations seemed surprised to get our call, as Christian parents pleading for help."

True.

Today there are books, Yellow-Page ads, and even professional advisers to help you examine options and make decisions. One of the best books I've seen is *How to Find Help for a Troubled Kid* by John Reaves and James Austin (Henry Holt, New York, 1990). Many parents find help by combining these resource materials with Christian referrals.

You discover you are not alone when you are searching. When your teen's crisis is past and you are going on with living, you discover again that you are not alone. The phone rings, a parent asks you for help. You share what you've learned. And another teen in crisis is helped.

Helping Resources for Teens

These lists are not intended to be complete, nor are they endorsements. I offer them in hope that they encourage you to begin your networking efforts to find help.

Military schools—Midwest (examples)
Culver Military Academy, Culver, Indiana
Howe Military Academy, Howe, Indiana
Northwestern Military Academy, Lake Geneva, Wisconsin
St. John's Military Academy, Delafield, Wisconsin

Institutional references for youth care (examples)
Independent Educational Consultants Association
Box 125, 38 Cove Road
Forestdale, MA 02644
(You can get a copy of the schools who are members of this organization by writing.)

New Horizons
1000 S. 350 East
Marion, IN 46953
1-800-458-9127
Institutional environment, dorm, and youth homes
Three facilities: Marion, Dominican Republic, and Canada (summers) Nondenominational, strict, highly structured, strong academic program (Students must earn rights.) 150 students

Mountain Park Baptist Academy
Patterson, MO 63956
314-856-4215
Primarily girls' school until recently; restrictive, highly disciplined, high security; must sign one-year contract; $650 per month.

Freedom Village
Lakemony, NY 14857
1-800-VICTORY

Institutional setting, agricultural; uses ACE educational program; 200 students; $650 per month.

Ray Swan
Hattiesburg, MS 39401
601-261-5152
Private, residential environment; strong family and local church support

Pregnancy Counseling
Crisis Pregnancy Center, Chicago, IL
Salvation Army, Chicago, IL
Evangelical Child and Family Services, Wheaton, IL

Self-help Organizations
Al-Anon Family Group Headquarters, Inc.
P.O. Box 862, Midtown Station
New York, NY 10018-0862

Big Brothers/Big Sisters of America
230 N. Thirteenth Street
Philadelphia, PA 19107
General Service Board of Alcoholics Anonymous, Inc.
P.O. Box 459
Grand Central Station
New York, NY 10163

Toughlove
P.O. Box 1069
Doylestown, PA 18901

— 9 —
When the Law Steps In: Intruding Arm or Helpful Hand?

Most kids know Officer Friendly. He visited their grade school, taught them about crossing streets, bike safety, and avoiding strangers. By junior high, Officer Friendly transforms a bit. The man in the dark blue uniform may be a security guard in the school, or a street officer who warned them to walk their dirt bike or carry their skateboard.

Many teens have little contact with police. An occasional speeding ticket may be the extent of their "record," if one exists at all. The picture changes drastically for some teens in crisis. A teen experiencing fireworks at home or underachieving at school may run away or cut school. Poor decisions while driving, violating curfew, or drinking may reveal a different side of Officer Friendly.

Parents of these teens are often in disbelief. I understand the feeling: "It can't be happening to us. Police cars are supposed to pull up to someone else's door, not ours."

But for some of us, the law stepped in.

If your teen is not involved with the law, this chapter may be one you can skip. Or you may want to read it in order to support other parents who find themselves working with juvenile officers, court dates, and decisions about whether to hire an attorney.

There are a few old truths that bear repeating and remembering for parents of teens in crisis, or for anyone who works with teens: youth workers, church leaders, and relatives.

- Any teen can indulge in occasional wrongdoing; that's part of being human.
- When teens do wrong, the parent's primary obligation is to make sure they are held responsible for their actions.
- Teens who are held accountable are less likely to repeat the wrong behavior.

Let's look at some crisis events for teens that frequently involve the law. Sometimes more information helps us make better decisions or at least choose the best option of those available.

School Truancy

Until age sixteen, kids are required by law to attend school. With parental permission, students between sixteen and eighteen can drop out of school before graduation. If a teen is between sixteen and eighteen and the parent refuses to sign withdrawal papers, it is unlikely that the law will step in. I will probably be criticized for saying that in print; however, that's the way it is in most counties. There simply are not enough truant officers to follow up on older students whose parents want them to stay in school when they refuse. Truancy officers concentrate on younger students.

If a student is under sixteen and misses 10 percent or more of the school's required 180 days, parents can be charged with a misdemeanor. In a recent conviction in Chicago, parents whose son missed ninety days were sentenced to one year of court supervision and ordered to pick up their son's report card and attend a conference with his teachers. The spokeswoman for the school system stated that their goal was not to prosecute parents but have children in school.

Some school districts have adopted policies that range from revoking students' licenses to reducing welfare payments as ways to force parents to keep their children in school. One parent, who preferred to remain anonymous, said, "I don't think it's fair. We buy him clothes, give him lunch money, and get him up and out the door. He just doesn't go. We've lost control. But he's lost interest. Isn't the school at fault too?"

If a parent gets frustrated and hits his or her teen, the boy or girl can dial 9-1-1. Then the police come, and the parent is in trouble. While the intentions of some of the laws are good and designed to prevent abuse, in many cases, they have backfired. Child advocacy laws have promoted child license. Control has moved from the parent to the child or teen's hand, and everybody loses.

If truancy is your teen's problem, it is unlikely that the law can help you beyond lecturing your teen. Parents are more likely to get help by considering a different school option like the ones mentioned in the last chapter.

I have observed a few cases where a family move has helped. In two cases where gang threats had forced kids to stay home, families moved to our district. Today both students are attending regularly and passing classes. We'll talk more about gang influences later. Family moves don't always have a happy ending, but those did.

Runaways

Most parents of teens can remember an argument that ended with their teen storming out the door in frustration and anger. Most return in minutes or hours, cooled down or hungry. Not all.

Typically teens walk for a while or visit a friend. Having space and time to cool off is not bad. Unfortunately, teens no longer have many safe places to cool off. I could run to the back of the farm and hide in the pines. Strange footsteps were four-legged creatures who were as afraid of me as I was of them. Today, not so.

More than a million teenage runaways roam the streets of America's major cities. Pimps lure one in three of these kids into prostitution within forty-eight hours after they have left home. Other runaways turn to thievery, petty or grand. Most act tough, but are, in fact, scared and vulnerable.

The picture is less bleak in suburbs and rural areas, but the problem is increasing.

Teens who run away from home have little concept of the implications of their actions. Most states have laws stating that a minor who leaves must be reported within twenty-four hours. When parents report their runaway, they are usually required to sign that, when the child is found, they will pick up him or her wherever found within twenty-four hours. Police are no longer allowed to detain a runaway minor in a juvenile facility.

Before 1974, minors whose acts would not be illegal if committed by an adult (like changing residences), were detained in secure juvenile facilities. These minors are called status offenders. In 1974 Congress decided to withhold federal funds from states that detained minors for status offenses. This frustrates police efforts to help runaways and parents' efforts to retrieve their children, and it makes running away more dangerous.

Though there is no typical runaway, most see themselves as leaving a stressful environment and escaping to a better life of freedom. Some leave families of substance abuse or sexual abuse. Many suffer from severe emotional problems or neurophysiological impairment or are substance abusers themselves. Some are kicked out of their homes. Others are looking for excitement or searching for themselves.

Statistics indicate that running away occurs more frequently from single-parent homes and among adopted children. Though most teens don't believe it, conditions on the streets are usually worse than home, and what they think will be freedom is a different kind of life.

As I reviewed books and articles on runaways, I found that most were written from the viewpoint of runaways or the people and agencies who try to help them. I didn't see much that was written from the parents' viewpoint. I understand. Parents whose kids have run away don't want to stand up and talk about it, or write about it. We are the bad guys.

With children who would consider going home, 68 percent of their parents responded, when called, that they didn't want their children back. This is heartbreaking for everyone. It is indeed tragic that being a parent has become so difficult and painful that many adults don't want to be Mom or Dad anymore. Many feel they just can't succeed. They feel they have failed at the job and don't want to try again.

Christian families are not immune. In fact, they have an added ingredient of stress. Our values are increasingly in opposition to our culture, so our rules and expectations are farther from what our teens are taught in every arena. We receive no reinforcement or support from society's institutions.

We are more aghast at the lyrics of music, sensitized to good and evil, and concerned for our children as eternal beings, temples of the Holy Spirit. Perhaps we feel more accountable. I don't know. I do know that it is more difficult to stand as a parent against something that society loudly says, "It's okay. It's the kid's decision." Our consciences say, "Not so!"

Children Become Accountable

I have been comforted by some truths from Scripture that

I had somehow not examined in relationship to teens before. At the age of twelve, Jesus explained to his family that he had to be about his Father's business (Luke 2:49). Of course, our teens' declarations and decision making are not necessarily Christlike; however, the principle is clear that children become accountable for their own actions. Age may vary. But somewhere in the early teens, kids make decisions for which they must answer. They begin choosing their directions—selecting their own gods or God. We cannot choose for them. At some point, we need to say that we taught them as well as we could and set the best example we could and must release them to make their life choices.

With that perspective, if they break the law, the "render to Caesar" principle applies. *Pay what you owe.*

Parents may need to evaluate how much support to give. For some, this means deciding whether to stand in court with their child regarding a speeding ticket. It may mean deciding whether to secure a lawyer when charges are more serious and/or numerous.

Driving under the influence of alcohol is usually an offense for which a license is revoked. Parents' first sense may be, "How will my kid get to work or to school with no wheels?" Parents must look at the bigger picture and say, "How will my teen learn accountability? If I continually step between my child and the law, how will my child learn boundaries?"

Many parents take a supportive position with the first offense. There are at least two good reasons to do this: (1) your teen then has evidence that you are on his/her side; and (2) the law and/or the system may be unreasonable or unfair.

Judges, police officers, and those in the bureaucratic hierarchy are human beings capable of bad decisions and mistakes, as well as overreactions. The "system" has its own baggage and bloopers that can complicate an already stressful situation. Hiring an attorney may avoid inappropriate consequences and help you work through the system. Teens can help pay the fees in addition to whatever consequence the court determines.

Precisely how far you go to help is a decision that only you can make. It helps to talk with other insightful parents. Collect good advice and encouragement. But no one else walks in your shoes, has lived in your family, and knows your resources, emotional and financial.

With great remorse, one parent lamented that she had gotten her son off for twelve DUIs. But in the thirteenth incident, someone died. Her son was the driver, but she felt responsible because she had shielded him too long. This mother had spent thousands of dollars for legal fees, and many years trying to protect her baby. She thought she was buying him time to get hold of his life. But another teen lost her life while he was trying to get hold of his.

Parental Restraint Has Limits

Accountable parenting is illustrated in Scripture and often taught and preached with great passion. When Hophni and Phinehas sinned, God called Eli to task for not restraining them (1 Samuel 2:27-29). Learning restraint begins at birth. An infant learns that the world was not created for her/his pleasure or control. I have talked to parents who feel that their teens have not yet learned that lesson. Here again, society sends a double message: "Any pleasure is okay. Control is okay, if you are the stronger, or you don't get caught." Today it is difficult for teens to learn to live with restraints.

If a child becomes a teen and the parents cannot control him or her, most states allow for the law to step in. Earlier I referred to Illinois' Minor Requiring Adult Intervention Provision. Stated simply, it means that if parents can no longer restrain a teen—they are abusive to others and out of control—the parent can take them or report them to local juvenile authorities and ask for intervention. As I mentioned before, this is seldom advertised and rightly so. Our overburdened juvenile justice system is not searching for clients. However, it is more frequently used as families have fewer resources of extended families and are under increased stress. The enticements to kids to be abusive and break the law are greater.

Parents often lack information on what help is available. In Illinois a legal services directory is published that lists free and low-cost legal services. Services are placed in categories such as guardianship and advocacy, rape victim services, and children and family services.* Often these resources can give counterpart addresses for other states. In the Chicago area, churches are increasingly providing excellent services for legal support and information. Rock of Our Salvation and Willow Creek Community Church are two of many. As a parent whose teen is in crisis, you may want to explore how these legal services can help as well as what local churches provide.

Legal Services Directory (Chicago: The Chicago Council of Lawyers and The Fund for Justice of the Chicago Council of Lawyers, 1988).

As I talked to parents whose teens have been involved with the law, they unanimously said to send this message: "When you first see signs that your child is moving out of control, act quickly!" Many felt that if they had responded more quickly while they still had some control, things might have been different. Some of their "if onlys" include the following:

- intervening with the public school at the first sign of lower grades
- changing to a private school, with a smaller setting, where monitoring and more support are available
- getting family counseling to learn to reduce stress earlier
- letting the kid pay for the speeding tickets and lose his license sooner
- talking to wise mentors sooner (swallowing your pride before you have to choke on it!)
- paying for the return trip ticket one time (after running away); after that, if they have the resources to leave, letting them find the resources to return (The prodigal son's dad did not go to get him; he watched and waited, see Luke 15:11-32.)

Parents of teens who had been involved with the law also made another point: listen to your inner feelings and doubts, and trust your eyes and ears. Some had denied or sidestepped evidence of problems that later rose up and smacked them in the face.

"By the time I heard my kid explain everything away,

I forgot what I asked him," one parent said sadly. Often teens deny the truth to their parents and even themselves. It's tough for anyone to face problems.

Speaking of tough problems, abuse is one of the most insidious to discover and to solve. It may be a part of the scenario of some teens in crisis.

Child Abuse Reporting

Laws were passed with good intentions to protect children, primarily from sexual and physical abuse. An adult who is informed by a child of sexual or physical abuse must report it. Public-school counselors can be sued if they do not report these alleged incidents. The intent of the law is good. Previously we could give that information to a designated party who could selectively decide what and when to report. Reporting is no longer optional.

Definition for suspected child abuse or child neglect: an abused or neglected child means a child whose physical or mental health or welfare is harmed or threatened with harm by acts or omissions by his parent or other persons responsible for his welfare.

After the report is made, our state law requires that the child and family agency make contact with the family within twenty-four hours to begin investigating the report. Depending on the findings of the investigation, either the child or abuser can be removed from the home.

The system is by no means unflawed. The Family Research Council in Washington, D.C., a division of Focus on the Family, has studied this issue and identified necessary changes. Children often experience greater harm and trauma when removed from their homes and placed in foster care. Many sources suggest that the extended family be the first option for care of children rather than foster care.

One girl described her terror at being suddenly removed from her home to a crowded home with sixteen other girls after sexual abuse was reported. Her stepgrandfather was the abuser, and he lived in a distant city. Her relatives could not get her out for days, though the abuser had left town and there were other safe places with relatives where she could live.

As a victim, she was victimized again by the system.

Mandatory reporting is appropriate. But appropriate solutions are far from available.

When a teen says that he or she has been hit by a parent, reporting is mandatory. There is considerable disagreement on this. Parents shouldn't strike a child in anger. However, this law has effectively taken away any physical methods of restraint by parents. A child or teen can call 911 and report a spanking or a swat. The police must respond and make a report.

I listened as a distraught girl described her dad's yelling and meanness. She displayed her black eye and described how he swung at her. As she wept, the black eye began to move down her cheek with her tears. As she blew her nose loudly, the tissue further moved her "black eye" across her nose and chin. I had to report her report. I also reported that the black eye had changed to a smudged face by the end of our talk.

Local agencies and hotlines can offer help for abused

kids, abused parents, and abusive parents. Communities are investing more in helping services, and I see a growing number of churches offering effective help. Teen harbors can provide an excellent safe place while kids and their helpers look for solutions.

Gangs

Increasingly, teens are being faced with making decisions about gang involvement. If you live in a large city and your kids are in public schools, they have already made decisions. In many suburbs, gangs are an option, though not a strong one. This is changing rapidly in many areas.

Parents often cannot understand why kids affiliate with an organization that, without exception, requires illegal and/or harmful behavior in some arena. The answer is an old cliché: *Kids want to be wanted.*

In many communities, the fastest growing gangs are in minority populations that are rapidly expanding at the same time that their families and cultures are being exposed to new stresses. For example, in a community where students from Mexico enter in growing numbers, the teens are ripe pickings for gang recruitment. In the old country, families were important, being together was important, and people connectedness was priority.

The family, or part of the family, moves. Mom and Dad are working two jobs at low wages to put food on the table or to bring Grandma or Uncle to the country of opportunity. Teens are less frequently supervised and often lonely. They may have little money and see lots of things they want. The gang offers them belonging, the feeling of family, support, and immediate acceptance.

Sounds good, doesn't it? Many gangs needn't recruit using fear. Gang bangers and "wanna be's" are plentiful. They want to be wanted.

Many parents feel powerless. They cannot provide money like gangs can. But we can continue to give all the love and encouragement we possibly can to our teens. And, in the long run, that is the most powerful incentive.

I do not think that individual families can resolve the gang problem. Even if love and lots of nurturing could keep a teen out of a gang, he might be killed as an innocent bystander. This is one of those problems that communities will need to unite to conquer. And some are doing it!

It's Not Over till It's Over

I have read the parable of the lost son (in Luke 15:11-32) many times recently. On one particularly gray, lonely morning, I let my imagination rewrite the script:

"I'm outta here," the young man said in his heart.

He took what could be called his—some cash, a vehicle—and left. He went to a place where no one would recognize him. He could always find a roof to sleep under as long as his money held out. No more broccoli and alarm clocks. Just fast food and fun.

Then a fun famine set in. It arrived when his money ran out. The partiers decided they'd rather party with someone else.

"Young man for hire," he advertised.

"You're hired," a city citizen said.

They called him the Deliverer. Errand Man.

First he delivered messages, then unidentified packages, then people. As long as he delivered, he got paid, and he could eat. But there was a gnawing hunger inside.

When the city citizen asked him to deliver death, he came to his senses.

He retraced his steps back home.

What drew him home? Not a free one-way ticket; not Mom's pleading voice; not bribes and promises; but the gnawing inside. He was hungry for home.

He no longer called out "give me." He cried, "Take me!" Then he was ready to come home.

The law can take your teen's freedom; the streets can take your teen's mind and body. But no one can take your teen's memories of what family is and what was good about home. The prodigal son came to his senses—and then he came home.

⏤ 10 ⏤

Drugs and Alcohol

The doorbell rang. It was 10:45 P.M. Brian was supposed to be home at 11:30. Mr. Simpson had dozed off in his armchair. Half awake, he opened the door to Brian's friend.

"Brian's in the car. He's sick."

> **Real life delivers stress and surprises. Drugs deliver reliable effects with little effort.**

The night was hot and muggy. Mr. Simpson was wide awake now. He hurried to the car. Brian was slumped in the backseat with a strange pallor. His damp shirt clung to his chest."Brian! Brian!" Mr. Simpson nudged him, then gently shook him. No response. He ran inside, awakened his wife, and called the paramedics.

Speed smeared the streetlights. Familiar neighborhood buildings blurred strangely. His thoughts leaped and scattered. He tried to collect them. *Carmen said Brian might have taken something. Yes, there were drugs at the party. Party? Brian hadn't said he was going to a party. He was going to the movies. This happens in the movies. Will Marge bring my wallet? Carmen said Brian took something bad. Carmen said? Carmen isn't saying all he knows!*

Brian's parents had hours to collect their thoughts at the hospital. They still could not put all the pieces together. Before they were sent home, the resident gently told them that Brian's stomach had been pumped. Since the circumstances were sketchy at best, it might have been an intentional overdose, a suicide attempt. He would be in intensive care for at least twenty-four hours. There was nothing more the Simpsons could do at the moment.

Brian had been admitted to a general hospital. Three days later, when the facts were evaluated and the blood tests completed, he was transferred to a sister hospital specializing in substance abuse. The Simpson's suspicions had been confirmed, and the crisis had forced a decision. Brian ended up in an appropriate place.

The news about drugs and alcohol is both good and bad. There has been a 44 percent drop in cocaine and illicit drug use since 1988. However, alcohol use is increasing, and kids are drinking at an earlier age. When your teen is in crisis and you suspect or *know* that drugs or alcohol are involved, statistics do not resolve your personal problem. However, information can help you see the broader picture and perhaps understand why it is so easy for teens to get involved. So here are the statistics:

- Ninety percent of high-school seniors have had experience with alcohol.
- Two-thirds have used it in the past month.
- One-third have had five or more drinks in a row on at least one occasion in the past two weeks.
- One-fifth of high-school seniors are daily smokers.
- One-fifth live with a chemically dependent parent.

Drug or alcohol use is like poison ivy. One little itchy bump seldom persists alone. Direct connections with reckless or lethal driving, pregnancy, law violations, and venereal diseases spread insidiously. When confronted with a crisis, often parents will look back and see the danger signs they wish they had heeded. If you see the following warning signs, don't ignore them:

Drugs and Alcohol: Signs that Spell Trouble
- Changes in school attendance, quality of work, grades, or discipline
- Unusual flare-ups or outbreaks of temper
- Withdrawal from responsibility
- General changes in overall attitude
- Deterioration of appearance and grooming
- Wearing sunglasses at inappropriate times
- Continual wearing of long-sleeved garments
- Association with drug users

- Turning away from former friends and activities
- Stealing from family, employer, or school
- Secretive behavior involving friends, phone calls, activities, and whereabouts
- Reduced motivation, self-discipline, and self-esteem
- Possession of large amounts of money or new, expensive items
- Greater susceptibility to colds, flu, etc.
- Use of drug paraphernalia, catalogs, T-shirts, belt buckles, and slogans

Returning to my office from an early morning meeting recently, I noticed a distraught-looking parent waiting to see a counselor. "He's here to see you," Dagne said. "He's been here since 7:20." In our offices, that is early for parents to arrive without an appointment unless they are upset.

He walked briskly into my office clutching a piece of paper that described his son's recent removal from a class. I reviewed Ric's downhill slide. Dad kept shaking his head saying, "I don't understand. I don't understand."

I decided to bluntly ask, "Do you think he's using something? Is he drinking?"

After a long pause with head bowed, he quietly murmured, "I must take him to a doctor."

We began to talk about options. The first step he had to take was the hardest.

What Every Family Can Do

1. *Face reality.* Every parent should know that his or her child will be exposed to drugs, from nicotine to heroin.

Every parent should know that no child is immune to temptation. Denial is an unsafe, unhealthy space that allows a teen to continue using drugs. It is a space for a child to learn greater manipulation skills or to develop his own denial pattern. Ric's dad had suspected the worst, but he had kept his questions to himself.

2. *Talk, talk, talk.* Set the stage for open communication. Hopefully you have talked about drugs before the teen years. But if not, begin where you are.

3. *Make prevention your goal.* Spell out family rules so your teens have guidelines on which to base their behavior. Spell out what will happen if the rules are broken. Help teens develop strong communication skills. They need to know it's okay to disagree or to express an opinion. If they can't communicate their feelings at home, they won't in peer groups either and will simply follow the crowd.

4. *Intervene quickly.* Ric's distraught dad made a phone call to a diagnostic center and confirmed a time to take his son for an evaluation. Ric did not know where they were going and would certainly have voted "No!" had he been asked. Interventions may range from limiting vehicle use to hospitalization. Since hospitalization is such a drastic and costly intervention, we'll spend a whole chapter on that subject. It is an option to be carefully considered.

Why My Teen?

I have never talked with a parent with a teen in crisis who did not ask the question, "Why *my* son?" "Why *my* daughter?" If we knew the precise answer to this question, we could probably prevent alcohol and substance abuse. We do not. But we *do* know some factors that indicate teens at risk.

The risk reasons may be present when the egg and sperm first unite, or they may develop through the growing-up struggle, or they may erupt over a single event in a teen's life.

The acronym D.R.U.G.S. spells out significant feelings in teens at risk.

D Despair—feeling hopeless and uncared for

R Revenge—feeling resentment over being rejected or dealt a "bad hand"

U Uncertainty—feeling unsure of who they are and how they are connected to family, school, or society

G Godlessness—feeling no sense of spirituality (yes, the secular professionals say this!)

S Skill deficits—feeling unable to move with confidence and competence in the world of family, friends, school, and work

When these underlying feelings meet with the following ten risk factors, the potential of abuse increases drastically.

1. Family history of alcoholism
2. Poor family management practices (including poorly defined expectations for behavior and inconsistent and excessively severe discipline)
3. Parental drug use and positive attitudes toward use
4. Academic failure beginning in late elementary school
5. A low degree of commitment to education

6. Alienation, rebelliousness, or lack of social bonding to others who are prosocial
7. Antisocial behavior in early adolescence or younger ages
8. Association with peers who use drugs
9. Favorable attitudes by teen toward drug use
10. Early initiation of drug use

When the underlying risk feelings combine with the risk factors, some chemical is available to every teen. Most teens, preteens, and grade schoolers can tell their parents who they could contact if they wanted to get drugs.

Why Some Teens Say No

The "Just Say No" campaign against drugs and alcohol has brought attention to our teens' crisis. But every parent and those of us working with teens know that the words are more easily said than lived. Those who say no have reasons. Here are answers teens give us that motivate them to resist:

- They are aware of the physical and emotional consequences of drug abuse and addiction.
- They have goals for themselves.
- They have positive role models at home.
- They have a strong religious background.
- They have clear expectations at home.
- They have a secure, positive self-concept.
- They have the skills to say no.
- They have good judgment and decision-making skills.

- They have other ways of having fun or letting off steam.
- They recognize the consequences of getting caught or getting in trouble at home.
- They have significant adults to whom they can turn.

Parents who suspect their teen is using drugs or alcohol need to ask lots of questions. Usually they need to get an objective outsider's opinion on what they are hearing. Some teens can tell you why they use drugs; others can't. Parents can combine the answers they are hearing with what they know of their teen. Since our parents' ears sometimes hear distortion, it's wise to involve someone else. Community counseling services often provide that objective outside party, who can hear more rationally.

In family therapy, Brian told his parents that he used to feel more like part of the group. Moving across the big city the previous year had been a minor move to Mr. and Mrs. Simpson. No job changes, just the opportunity to rent a house, not an apartment.

But Brian didn't know how to make a new set of friends and adjust to a new school schedule at the same time. Some kids can and some can't. To treat only Brian's addiction would not solve the problem. Many parents and teens have learned the hard way that treating the addiction only provides an interlude in abusing, not the cure.

The addiction and the *cause* of the addiction must be addressed. Treatment centers are recognizing the need for dual diagnosis—treating the "what" *and* the "why." Ignoring this fact is the reason for the dismal success rate for teens after one hospitalization or treatment center stay. About half are clean one year later according to the more encouraging statistics. Some studies indicate only one-fourth stay straight. This is a dismal statistic that translates to kids in a repeat crisis, and to parents who are often dismayed and financially depleted. It is not unusual for a teen (or adult for that matter) to make a return trip to deal with their addiction.

One follow-up study of youths a year after their stay in a treatment center (thirty-five-day average) indicated the following:

- 22 percent said things were going better than ever
- 45 percent reported some improvement
- 33 percent said things were about the same or worse

Most of the teens in the survey were living with their parents (49 percent of the original sample). We can logically assume from what we know of teens who do not live with their parents that this sample illustrates the more positive results of treatment. Most were referred to continuing care groups, halfway houses, or private therapy; 68 percent followed through with this recommendation; 37 percent remained clean after their discharge from treatment; 28 percent of those who used again were rehospitalized.

Of those who relapsed, their stated reasons were: (1) testing personal control (adults who relapsed stated this also as the number one reason); and (2) social pressure (adults stated negative emotional states as the number two reason). Female teens had a higher recovery rate than male teens. Teens who participated in self-help or continuing care activities after discharge had higher rates of recovery than those who did not.

This is important information for parents to know. In crisis we want to believe in any available solution. Treatment centers for substance abuse are helpful. They provide teens a dry, safe space to absorb information about themselves and their addiction. But the stamp "Discharged" on the final bill does not mean "Cured."

Informed parents can examine the causes they suspect in their teen and address them. While no parent can say no for his teen, addressing the cause gives the teen support when *he* chooses to say no.

How Parents Can Help

1. *Help your teen develop problem-solving skills.* When she faces a problem, talk through options and solutions. Use the four-step "Coping with a Problem" technique that I've included. Sit down together (at a restaurant if home is too distracting) and write the pros and cons of each option.

2. *Focus on internal worth.* Americans seek external worth: money, appearance, and competition. Reinforce your teen's internal worth: being special because God created him. Your son or daughter is important to *you*, period.

3. *Reduce chronic stress in the household.* Stress-free living is impossible. But a household out of control is an invitation for any member to want to "numb out." Resolve conflicts by speaking up assertively, negotiating,

and managing family affairs. Otherwise, the demands of modern life seem overwhelming.

Coping with a Problem

Step 1: Look honestly at the problem. Write it down. Ask yourself, "What is really happening?"

Step 2: Think of several ways to deal with this problem or situation. Brainstorm. Write down the possible solutions.

Step 3: Weigh the pros and cons for each solution. If you have two options, rule a paper in four sections. Option #1: pros/cons. Option #2: pros/cons. Seeing it in writing often crystalizes your thinking.

Step 4: Decide what you are going to do, and act.

Step 5: (optional) Tell someone who can hold you accountable if you fear backing out of your decision.

---

4. *Plan family activities to overcome feelings of isolation.* One family's after-care assignment was to have a movie/pizza night to get them in the same room—an event that had not happened for months. With fewer intact families, looser community ties, and lack of intimacy, loneliness is widespread in teens. While you cannot be their buddy, you *are* their family.

5. *Handle competition and goal orientation cautiously.* While having personal goals is a reason teens say no, becoming goal-driven and motivated only to compete rather than work for personal or higher principles results in a too-demanding life-style. As parents we can fall into the trap and set an example of striving for perfection. Christian parents are especially susceptible. We forget that Jesus took time to get out on the lake away from the crowds, enjoyed dinner parties, and got alone in order to be refreshed.

6. *Step out of that place between your teen and those who are holding her accountable for her behavior.* The line between parenting a child and "enabling" a teen is fine and fragile. If *your* parents and family were dysfunctional and/or you know you have boundary difficulties, you may need outside help in parenting.

7. *Take advantage of self-help groups.* Groups such as Al-Anon and Al-Ateens have a terrific track record for helping families in crisis. Many families have leaned heavily on church youth groups. Just talking with family, friends, and others is tremendous therapeutic help. Parents get ideas and feel less isolated. They discover not only that they are not alone, but that there is hope in the future.

8. *Ask your teen about ideas on ways to say no.* Get his or her opinion on the following ways to say no to a drink or any substance:

- No, thanks, I'm driving.
- No, thanks, it's just not me.
- No, I usually end up embarrassing myself.
- No, I don't like the taste.
- No, what else have you got?
- No, I'm in training (or I don't want to gain weight).
- No.

Your teen may discover a refusal skill. You will have had an opportunity for conversation. And you'll know your teen a bit better by listening to his or her responses.

Before closing this chapter, I feel compelled to encourage you to take care of yourself. You may need to skip to chapter 13 for support. Though substance-abusing teens are needy and draining, do not neglect yourself. Their demands may become so great that you feel as needy and drained as they are. Chapter 13 will give lots of specifics, but for now remember that Jesus told us to love our neighbor as we love ourselves. Love your teen as you love yourself. You are loved and lovable. Treat yourself that way.

~ 11 ~

Hospitalization: The Popular Option of the '90s

My husband and I pulled into the hospital parking lot. This November day seemed grayer than Chicago's bleakest days. The walk from the car to the entrance seemed longer than ever before. The wind somehow penetrated our bones. I had come to this psychiatric hospital many times to visit my students and had walked briskly with a light step into the attractive foyer. Today was different.

We reached for each other's hand in an uncanny simultaneous motion as we approached the desk.

"Two South-B, please?" My husband's voice sounded strained.

Through the great doors, up the elevator. Buzzed into a waiting area, identified to the floor supervisor, escorted through another floor, buzzed into another section. The therapist opened another door.

Our son.

Prayed for, waited for, applied for, and loved in the best way we knew how. He had delighted us, entertained us, and expanded our lives. But grope as we might in our past experiences, we could find no comfort big enough to fill this gaping hole.

He looked different. It was not the orange jumpsuit—though that was strange. It was as though all the subtle changes of the last year surfaced in the questioning look with which he greeted us. Who was this young man? Son? Stranger? This was not small Sonnyboy as we affectionately called him as we tousled his white-blond hair. This was not our Little Man, as his aunt's nanny, Miss Christy, nicknamed him—the small, quiet gentleman at the rowdy table of all the cousins.

We would get to know this young stranger. His survival literally depended on it.

Baring our private, family soul is painful. But we have committed together to do so, with our son's permission, to encourage others. We felt so alone struggling through this crisis. When we gained the strength to talk, we found incredible support and comfort by sharing our load of grief. Because we are believers we are instructed to bear each other's burdens. "Share each other's troubles and problems, and so obey our Lord's command. If anyone thinks he is too great to stoop to this, he is fooling himself. He is really a nobody" (Galatians 6:2-3).

Psychiatric hospitalization is a burden that, from our experience, is impossible to bear alone. In the past, some might have considered it one of those "private" problems. Paul talks in Galatians about those loner problems: "Each of us must bear some faults and burdens of his own. For none of us is perfect" (Galatians 6:5). The analogy is to a soldier's backpack, one's personal accountability backpack, that weighs about sixty pounds—a bearable load for one person.

Your child in crisis, your adolescent at risk, the crumbling of your son's or daughter's world is like a five-hundred-pound backpack. I fear that pride keeps some parents carrying this burden alone. It is humbling to reveal your failures, weaknesses, and the family flaws that are exposed in crisis. I understand.

Some carry the burden to avoid gossip and prejudice. I hope what I share will displace prejudice with compassion, gossip with support. Others, even in the body of believers, often fear what they don't understand. Perhaps all can learn from our pain and be instructed through our experience.

Dear parent reader, it is unlikely that you will experience what we have. I pray that you don't. If you are reading this book because you work with adolescents— perhaps you are a youth pastor, a camp supervisor, or a house parent—I write this to help you understand, reach out, and help carry the burden.

Why?

The number one reason that parents consider hospitalization for their adolescent is safety. Counselors, social workers, and others of us in the helping professions increasingly see kids putting themselves in positions of real danger. Running away when I was a child meant sprinting for the back of the farm in anger and huddling cold in the pine grove. When I shivered in the chill night air from fear, the hoot of an owl concealed by darkness and the shuffling of pine needles for unknown reasons raised goose bumps on my flesh.

It's not like that today. The streets welcome runaways in a different way from the pine grove. The sounds are not God's creatures, and the shuffler is not likely to be a nocturnal coon or possum.

Running away is a symptom, a behavior that says life is out of balance. Internal and/or external controls are not functioning. The frightened teen doesn't see the consequences we discussed in chapter 9 or feel the full fear that will set in later. Hospitals are a safer place, a locked facility where the decision to run is not an option, a setting where people will work with the teen on increasing internal positive control.

Attempting suicide is another common reason that teens are hospitalized. Some enter at the time of the attempt or when intent has been revealed by a family member or friend. Assaults and other threatening behavior may mean that hospitalization should be considered, either for the safety of the teen or those around him/her.

Irrational behavior may be a reason for hospitalization, although outpatient resources, including counseling, are usually a better first option unless safety is involved.

Substance abuse is the most common reason for hospitalization. We are increasingly acknowledging that this is not a cause in itself; rather, a dual diagnosis includes the substance abuse and *other factors*. Treating substance abuse alone is unlikely to bring balanced, healthy living. Statistics included in the last chapter indicate that up to one-third of teens hospitalized for substance abuse are readmitted.

While parents and those of us in the helping professions speak of reasons in behavioral terms (attempting suicide, running away, aggressive assaults, or irrational behavior), teens are admitted to hospitals based on categories of diagnosis. If you are a parent sitting across the desk from a psychiatrist who recommends hospitalizing your child, it is helpful to know the diagnostic terms— what he or she says is wrong with your child.

Most parents don't need to be convinced that there is a problem. (You know that by the time you arrive at the point of listening to a diagnosis.) But you are probably thoroughly confused by your child's behavior. You have been trying to figure out what's going on inside his head for days, weeks, or months. And you are probably physically and emotionally exhausted due to a recent crisis.

**Why Adolescents Are Admitted
to Psychiatric Hospitals**

These are the most common diagnostic categories:
   Affective psychoses
   Schizophrenic disorders
   Neurotic disorders
   Drug or alcohol dependence
   Personality disorders
   Conduct disorders
   Depressive disorders
   Adjustment reaction

When adolescents are admitted to psychiatric hospitals, they are diagnosed; a label is put on their behavior.

Usually the label is one of the eight diagnostic categories listed on page 183. It is truly difficult to describe behavior that a parent might observe for each category. Some behavior fits any of several. The adolescent who runs away may be depressed and looking for a high to cover his pain; he may be psychotic and believe he will be a star in Hollywood; or he may be using drugs and a gang is pressing him to pay up. Diagnosis is not an exact science, although tools and methods are becoming more precise.

We pored over the *Diagnostical and Statistical Manual of Mental Disorders** to understand our son's diagnosis. Not only did this book increase our understanding of his treatment, it also highlighted the importance of our giving the treatment staff as much information as possible about the months leading to hospitalization.

Hospitalizing difficult kids is not new. Originally, private mental hospitals were intended to alleviate scandal, not provoke it. "Incorrigible" teenagers—truants and runaways—were placed in adult jails or juvenile detention centers. Conditions were frequently horrendous. The Juvenile Justice and Delinquency Prevention Act of 1974 discouraged states from locking teens up. In the process of being deinstitutionalized, they were trans-institutionalized—shifted from the legal to the medical forum. Fresh concerns surfaced. Dr. Helen Beiser, a Chicago psychiatrist, summarized the concerns of some: "We have to decide what society does with adolescents who cause trouble—with people who just annoy others, people who in one way or another don't get along.

*Diagnostical and Statistical Manual of Mental Disorders, 3d ed., rev. (American Psychiatric Association, 1987, Washington, D.C.)

There's not much to be done for them in jail. I'm not sure any more is done in hospital stays."

From my perspective as a parent, our son's hospital experience was positive. From my experience as a counselor, I have seen instances where hospitalization was positive, neutral, or negative. Success is tied to an accurate diagnosis.

Children and adolescents suffer from schizophrenia as do adults. Increasingly, evidence points to genetic predisposition as the source of this illness. Medication can make reasonable, healthy living an option for 60 percent of those who suffer from this disease, if diagnosed and treated early. Fifteen percent will not suffer later, and 15 percent are severely ill beyond medical help at this time. When acting out becomes extreme, and hallucinating and lack of orientation to reality persist, hospitalization may be necessary and schizophrenia may be the diagnosis.

Adolescents also suffer from manic-depressive disorders. Referred to as bipolar, this disorder is characterized by extreme depression and extreme manic moods. While ups and downs are part of most adolescents' daily experience, a teen with bipolar disorder swings wildly out of control. Hospitalization may be needed for accurate diagnosis and monitoring of medication until accurate treatment is in place. This disorder is sometimes confused with adolescent depression, especially when caring adults are unaware of the teen's manic acting out.

The good news about bipolar is that medication (Lithium) is available to level out extreme mood swings. I am aware of students on Lithium who live in their homes and function in public schools, leading balanced and satisfying lives. Hospitalization may be one step in the treatment process.

Drug or alcohol dependence is the most frequent cause for hospitalizing teenagers. Forty percent involve drugs only or primarily, 27 percent used primarily alcohol, and 33 percent used both before entering treatment programs. Since these programs have been scrutinized for many reasons, not the least of which was insurance coverage, we have a growing body of information on their effectiveness.

Hospitalization is not a magic wand to solve all problems. I wish it were! It is an intervention to throw a probing searchlight on the problem. Medical issues may be diagnosed and psychological problems exposed. Treatment may be prescribed, and healing may begin.

But discharged does not mean cured.

In considering the reasons for hospitalization, it is significant that four out of five of these young people are white and most are middle or upper class. In parents' exasperated search for help, hospitalization may not be an alternative for some teens who could profit from it. Insurance coverage may be inadequate. Hospitalization may be a financial impossibility. We need more alternatives to help adolescents and their families in crisis when funds and/or insurance is limited.

Adolescents who have been hospitalized have interesting perspectives on the reasons for their experience. One student told me that her family would not confront her pain and her problems until she was hospitalized. Some welcome the distancing from home and school.

Some are not getting along with anyone. Others seem okay in one place but not another.

I have met with parents who are shocked to hear what their child has done in someone else's home, a mall, or a parking lot. They say, "He goes in his room as soon as he walks in the door," or "She sleeps a lot."

Cindy's family just couldn't accept that she needed help beyond what they could give. "When my parents came to see me in the hospital, they finally admitted I wasn't making it. For that matter, the whole family wasn't making it."

Most adolescents have a different perspective when they are released, and many feel they are doing better. Rumors bother them, but many acknowledge there were rumors before they were hospitalized. Many feel they have "grown up a lot" and somehow have entered a level of self-understanding that other adolescents do not have. This may not be the result of hospitalization alone. I think our son's self-understanding is the combined living experience of events and behavior leading to hospitalization, reentering his world again afterwards, and making it. Teens who have been hospitalized have been forced to analyze themselves, their relationships, and their behavior. Their survival depended on it.

Making the Decision

Dear Somebody,

Help! Help! Help! Can't anybody out there help me? I'm going into the hospital tomorrow, I'm

*scared. What is it like? Why are my parents doing
this to me? What will the other kids be like? I'm not
crazy; are they? All I want is to stay here in my
room. Please? Somebody Help Me!*

Cindy's mother showed me this letter she found in
Cindy's room the afternoon after they admitted her to an
adolescent psychiatric unit of a general hospital. Mom
was confused, exhausted, and also scared. She rehashed
the last days and then the past months. She cried, not the
first tears she had shed in my office. I met Cindy's parents
shortly after Cindy entered our high school. Attendance
problems were followed by avoiding behavior that Mom
and Dad felt helpless to deal with. They were caring
parents with two younger children who had exhausted
their information and emotions on how to parent their
bright teenage daughter.

On the days they could get her to go to school, she
spent lots of time in the nurse's office. She had headaches, stomachaches and anything-else aches. The nurse
would call home; Mom would dutifully come to school
to bring her home.

Their therapist said, "No more leaving school."
Maybe a firm approach would condition her to staying a
full day. Then Cindy's illness became dramatic. She
clung to the classroom doorway. She lay down in the hall.

Hospitalizing Cindy was far from an easy decision
for these parents. Their expressive extended family ar-
gued, mused, advised, and nagged. They worried about
how other kids would react, not just to Cindy, but her
brothers also. With limited insurance coverage for such

an expense, signing the payment plan to pay $12,000 over five years increased their internal pressure. We might think that as they left the hospital that morning, they would be relieved to have made the decision, completed the intake procedures, and said their temporary good-byes. Not so. These parents were unaware of the geraniums lining the parking lot, the rich autumn colors of the maples lining the river's edge. They walked to their car blinded by inner turmoil, still wondering if they had done the right thing.

Cindy's parents are not alone. In 1971, according to the National Center for Health Statistics, about 6,500 children and teenagers were hospitalized in private psychiatric facilities in the United States. In-patient hospitalization had increased to 82,000 in 1980, 112,000 in 1986, and 150,000 in 1989. One conservative estimate for 1991 was 250,000. I am not surprised to hear that adolescent psychiatric hospitals are sprouting all over the nation. These treatment centers are more likely to operate with black ink while many other hospitals are turning red.

The growing multi-billion-dollar adolescent psychiatric business is the result of the combined facts of the changes in our teenagers' world. Families are vastly different today from fifteen years ago. Parents face more problems with less support and fewer resources.

Hospitalization is an option that an increasing number of parents are considering to help them face problems with adolescents. Let's look at the issues that parents face when they consider this alternative. The diagnosing psychiatrist will offer some information. Relatives and co-workers will likely offer more. But the bottom line is that

Mom and Dad or one parent alone must make the final decision.

Which Hospital?

Hospitals for adolescents come in many shapes and sizes, from general to highly specialized, and, I would also add, with different levels of effectiveness. Drug and alcohol treatment facilities and psychiatric care will be our focus. They may be free-standing facilities, part of general hospitals, or a myriad of other combinations.

The concept is not new. One Chicago hospital opened as an alcohol and drug abuse treatment center during the Civil War when soldiers came home hooked on morphine, cocaine, and alcohol. In the 1980s, many hospitals began to use drug abuse programs to balance their books because insurance companies would readily pay for them though they were cutting back payments for other medical services. Now insurance companies are starting to look at those costs the same way they did at medical/surgical costs. Adolescent psychiatric units are the new black ink item fueled by health insurance dollars from middle-class families in crisis.

The critics, and there are always critics, say there are too many in this business and that some are in it only for the money. Medical/surgical units exist to make a profit. We don't avoid them because they are not philanthropic. We use them to take advantage of the services we need that they can adequately provide. Some adolescents need what some hospitals offer. Parents need information to help them make the best decision in choosing the right facility.

If your family or your teenager is already receiving counseling or in therapy, you have two benefits: that resource and time.

Ask the resource which hospital they recommend and use. Assuming you have met with a therapist or counselor, does he or she have a grasp of the problem? What is his or her recommendation? What does your common sense tell you about that recommendation? You may feel inadequate to deal with your child's problem. However, you are the best expert on that child even though you don't feel like it at the time! What do *you* think?

You may know others whose adolescent has been hospitalized, or your friends may know them. Diplomatically explore whether they will talk with you. We found them not only willing to answer our questions, but eager to be a support network. They will tell you the pluses and minuses of their experience. Use this information to select what hospital you will entrust with your child.

One parent wished that she had chosen differently. Her son was admitted to the hospital his therapist recommended. This hospital did not include parents in the treatment plan during hospitalization and did not recommend an after-care plan. Additionally, the cost was higher than others in our area. When her son had a relapse one month later, she was angry. She did not know what was going on, her financial resources were exhausted, and she had nowhere to turn. She wished she had asked questions earlier.

Ask your church for recommendations. Wisely analyze this information. Some pastors do not know the issues or may even stand in opposition to counseling and hospitalization. But they may be able to help you make a decision or refer you to those who can help.

If you have worked with your child's school, a counselor, social worker, or the school psychologist might offer some suggestions. Speaking as a high-school counselor, we do not say, "I recommend . . ." But we may suggest that the person check out certain facilities. Our school psychologist has worked with students treated at a variety of hospitals; some simply have a better track record than others. Sort and compare the information from your school. You may at least learn the strengths of different adolescent hospitals in your area.

Don't be afraid to critically evaluate. You are entrusting your eternal, priceless, impressionable, and fragile child to other people.

We sat in a lovely office across a polished table from the psychiatrist who had evaluated our son. We probably appeared like confident professionals—our feelings were mismatched in this situation. Having come from work in our business suits, we contrasted with our creatively dressed son in the waiting area. He wore black, black, and more black—combat boots, oversized trench coat, baggy pants, T-shirt. This particular day he was also wearing a heavy gold chain with a six-inch long cross dangling at his chest. We listened intently as this highly recommended director of the adolescent psychiatric floor of a reputable hospital gave his diagnosis. It made sense. So did his recommendation. But we chose a different resource.

A Christian clinic in our area evaluated our son. The

diagnosis and recommendation were similar. We chose the Christian clinic, knowing that their treatment objective would include encouraging our son's relationship with Jesus Christ.

I am grateful that Christian families have professional Christian resources—therapists, clinics, and hospitals. Distance may be a disadvantage, but for us that disadvantage was tiny compared to the benefits.

In crisis or tragedy, your child may be admitted to the nearest trauma center. That may be the wrong place for the kind of treatment your son or daughter needs. Within the first forty-eight hours, parents can request that their child be released to a different hospital. I know a single mother who exercised this right because her employer was willing to cover more of the costs at a different facility. The hospital to which her daughter was moved was, in my estimation, superior anyway. And the parents were better able to cope with the bills—not an unimportant benefit when all resources, including physical and emotional, are stretched to the limit.

Get thorough information on what everything will cost. Hospitalization is likely to be over $500 per day and may be nearer $1,000. Expenses include the facility, a physical examination, possibly medication, diagnostic tests that may be physical and psychological, and the costs of a psychiatrist and a team of therapists. You have to swallow the financial pill now or later.

During Hospitalization

I wish I could offer profound words to parents while their kids are in the hospital. "Hang in there" keeps coming to my mind. And that is neither profound nor spiritual. What I mean is, "Keep going, keep going, and keep going."

Keep going to the hospital. Take advantage of all the therapy and family groups you can. You will learn about your child in a way that would be impossible if he or she were not hospitalized. You will learn about yourself, your parenting, and the others in your family. You'll learn about your parents and maybe even your grandparents. Learn all you can. When you bring your teenager home, no matter how many therapy sessions you have fought or wept through, no matter how many artsy-craftsy things you have concocted with your child, no matter how many lectures you have heard—you will not know enough.

Keep going as a family. You will probably fight with your spouse and maybe even with your other kids. We did and it was terrible. We felt vulnerable, exposed, and helpless. The good news is that those are ripe conditions for change. We told our other children that we would try to prevent our son's crisis from affecting them. Soon we had to apologize and admit that we could not keep that commitment. They *were* affected. They were home alone many nights while we were at the hospital. We were always tired and could not meet their needs as we had before.

They survived on fast-food dinners, and we drank lots of coffee from Styrofoam cups on the tollway while we drove. Their friends knew that something different was happening in our home. They were affected when our family changed—and some of that was good.

We accepted with gratitude our friends' help. My husband opened an envelope from a coworker and friend.

The note promised prayer and suggested using the enclosed money for gasoline. We accepted both with tears of gratitude.

Our friends, the Johnsons, invited us for dinner one Saturday night. Their calm home seemed like an oasis in a storm. We had never tasted such a wonderful spinach salad. Seconds offered were speedily accepted. There were no leftovers after we finished the main course. And then there was coffee—in china cups and swallowed leisurely—with laughter and fellowship. That night of caring had unmeasured value to our frazzled souls and bodies.

Keep going, dear family, keep going.

Keep going as individuals. Actually my husband and I were both happy to have to work. There is comfort in the familiar routine, commuting to work, opening the mail, becoming immersed in the projects and problems of the job. Our minds were diverted. I looked forward to my three-mile run with greater than usual anticipation. Pounding the pavement became a welcome release of frustration. I left lots of worries along the course, and sleep came easier.

My husband thought perhaps he should skip playing racquetball. We agreed that other things were dispensable, but not this exercise. It was good for his mind as well as his body. (I would guess that he was a fierce competitor during those weeks!)

We gave up a clean living space, shopping for anything but survival necessities, reading the newspaper, and being hospitable. But we survived.

Keep going when your child comes home. I did not know that a temporary relapse is to be expected within the first month after hospitalization. Not knowing this, when our son fell apart his second week back at school, we thought we were back to square one. We were involved in an after-care treatment plan—and still it happened. Keep doing the best you can. I wish we had asked more questions about adjusting to the "outside world." Hospitalization is not a cure; it is a beginning.

Home Again, Home Again

Coming home has its special challenges. Here are two invaluable bits of advice that I was given for our family.

Though you wish to block out the memories of this painful time period, *don't forget the lessons learned.* Our therapist helped us get in touch with our child's feelings. I learned to hear our son as never before and feel with him more deeply than before our days of crisis. Although the process was painful, I want to always remember those lessons that helped me feel with my son.

Our pastor advised us to *set boundaries* when our son returned home from the hospital experience. That advice was puzzling at the time. Now I understand. What a valuable insight. After such a crisis, it is easy to focus on your child and his needs, his moods, his impending challenges. I told our therapist that I felt as though I was walking on eggs! As much as you care for your child, you must move toward regular living, rediscover your marriage, and attempt to return to balanced living. Your troubled adolescent is not the center of the universe. You may have lived as though he or she was for a while. But for your good as well as your child's, living needs to become balanced.

Teens are never the same after hospitalization—neither is your family, nor are you as a parent. Your ever-changing family mobile has gyrated wildly and will settle into a new configuration. While we felt fragile in readjusting, in fact, we found new strength. New boundaries soothed the gyrations and we began to face a new, and, I believe, *better* future.

I write this chapter one week after Mother's Day. It was a poignant day. As I sat at our dining-room table, I became acutely aware that my children were all alive. One year ago, I took that fact for granted. Not now. The day spent, the house quiet, my son called me to his room. I sat in the dark on the floor at his bedside.

"Mom, remember before I came, you told God you would take someone with a problem? And then you got me and found out I had crossed eyes. You thought that was the problem?"

"Yes, I remember." Though I could see the shadow of his two-hundred-pound frame, in my mind's eye, I saw my baby, smiling up at me, one eye focused, the other wandering. He was such a huggable cuddler. I would wrap him up in my arms and he would melt right into my neck. I did not doubt then that God would guide us through whatever was needed for our son to be whole.

"Mom. It just came to me. There was more. I think this was the problem God knew about." (He was referring to his being bipolar.)

"I think you're right, Son." Our voices sounded so quiet. So much had happened. "It's not what I expected."

"I love you, Mom. Happy Mother's Day."

— 12 —

Adoption: Love Isn't Enough

We were young and idealistic. Our Walden Pond was hardly as picturesque as Thoreau's retreat, but the cabin beside a Wisconsin lake was our dreaming post. We'd have a few children, and then we'd adopt a few more. If God gave us health and the strength to work, we would parent children whose biological parents could not.

Twenty-seven years later, we have four. Our daughter, Valerie, 21, was born to us. John, 18, was adopted. Charles, 16, was born to us. Robb, 14, was adopted.

Adoption, not abortion, the placards read.

I agree.

But there is a lot more to it.

Adoption.

There are two sides.

The ideal. The better idea. The philanthropic feeling. A cause. A philosophy of life and conception. A willing commitment. An adventure. An emotion-expanding, life-changing experience of love.

Adoption is more. Adoption is committing 157,680 hours to the unknown. It is twenty-four hours a day, seven days a week, fifty-two weeks a year, eighteen years minimum. And I mean minimum because parenting an adopted child lasts a lifetime, just as parenting a child born to you. When you make this commitment, you do not know what you are committing to. Would you sign a contract with none of the blanks filled in? Adoptive parents have.

Your experience may be like the glowing, love-filled stories in magazines with glossy pictures of smiling parents playing with healthy children on the playground. Or it may mirror the interracial families who experience a richness and diversity because of the new person in their lives.

Some families with adopted children are different. Forty percent of the adolescents in psychiatric hospitals are adopted children. Adopted children make up 2 to 3 percent of the population of children, but 27 percent of children who have Attention Deficit Disorder. Many sources cite higher incidence of Fetal Alcohol Syndrome or Fetal Alcohol Effect for adopted children. More than statistics, these are people—families, children, and adolescents who live daily with struggles that they did not dream could exist. While surprised or stunned by the struggle, we are usually unprepared with coping skills and information.

These families experience all the turmoil that families experience with adolescents born to them. Plus. They also live with a greater likelihood of increased turbulence in self-discovery and less resource information about the roots of the children's behavior. They live with greater likelihood of poor fit between family members. When they begin to talk about their experiences, to reach out for understanding, the dialogue goes something like this:

"She's so different. I can't understand how she can live in that room! And Sam's just the opposite. I feel like I should be two completely different mothers to parent them both!"

The listener, likely a parent with children born to her, says, "I understand. No two kids could be more different than my own. I know exactly what you mean."

Thinking she has comforted her friend, she has helped close a door of loneliness. Children born to a couple, though quite different, are products of the same genetic pool. Any resulting combination will have more similarities than two people created from separate genetic pools. Birth siblings at a family reunion, though as different as black and white sheep, will see or hear about someone who has a tiny resemblance to them in some way. Adopted siblings know there is no direct thread to anyone, no matter how big the family reunion!

Because there are many adopted children who become adults without crisis, who are comfortable about being adopted, it is sometimes mistakenly believed that adoption per se is not the problem. If it were, wouldn't all adoptees struggle?

Applying what we know of temperaments, genetic predisposition, and goodness of fit, being adopted affects different children in different ways. I've talked to parents whose adopted children sailed through adolescence like a catamaran. But then, upon the birth of their own children, depression set in, relationships became strained, and the new grandparents were stunned. The catamaran transformed into a sinking rowboat.

Since every adopted person is different, every family they enter varies, and life experiences don't fit prescribed formulas, we cannot provide an outline or grocery list of "Five Stages of Adopted Kids" or "Ten Happenings in Adoptive Families." But we can describe events that will be different and special issues for adopted adolescents. And we can share what has helped adoptive families emerge from struggling survival to success.

Events

Happy Birthday!

Dad aims the movie camera. Mom holds the cake just out of reach. Your one-year-old star coos, laughs, and drools to everyone's delight. After singing and cake cutting, baby is filmed plastering frosting on his cheeks and swiping his ear. Grandma laughs. The celebration shouts, "We're glad you were born!"

Years pass. Caring, knowledgeable parents tell their child, in the best way they know how, that he is adopted. Each year they celebrate that special day. As his mind matures, another message crowds in on birthdays. *This was not a happy day for someone. Someone out there dreaded this day. Someone did not want me to be.*

Birthdays can be tough for adopted kids. Our two adopted sons are as different as east and west. They seldom talk together about anything, least of all, adoption. However, on John's eighteenth birthday, John and Robb huddled in the back of the van during a long drive and shared feelings, questions, and "what if" stories. They spoke of fantasies and "what might have beens."

Birthdays are special events that feel different when you are adopted.

People who study adopted people have listed events that take on special or different significance: the birth of your own child, becoming the age of your biological mother or father when you were born, marriage, or the death of adoptive parents. Any loss. Loss is painful to all; however, adopted persons sense loss differently and sometimes more intensely. This varies with age of adoption, what happened between birth and adoption, and temperament. Adoptees are especially loss-sensitive.

Some events take on significance because of a comment or unexpected discovery: family reunions where no one looks "just like me"; a trip to the doctor where he thoughtfully looks at parents and says, "Now this acne will probably proceed like it did with one of you. Genetic tendency, you know." And then we must say that he's adopted. We were in the dark again, at a loss for how to empathize. When our daughter reached five-feet-eight-inches at age eleven, I understood why she stooped. I did, too; it had happened to me. It took me a while to understand why John wanted long hair to cover his blossoming forehead. It had not happened to me.

A typical school assignment of drawing the family tree is usually a painful event for adopted children. Which family tree does she draw? Her Asian grandparents or her adoptive Jewish grandparents?

There is another category of that doesn't exist for nonadopted people: meeting one's biological parents or siblings. These moments touch adopted people deeply, though they may not be able to express what they feel.

Usually these events do not become crises, but their accumulation may build beyond a teen's comfort zone. Just like all adolescents, adopted kids must work through the developmental tasks of growing up. In addition, however, they must integrate the fact of their adoption.

Special Issues

The serenity prayer asks God to help us change what we can change, accept what we cannot change, and know the difference between the two. Mature adults have trouble with this. Imagine being an adolescent adopted person, trying to find serenity . . .

Three special issues stir in adolescent teens that have potential for becoming storms:

1. *Identity:* Who am I? Where am I going? Would it help to know where I came from?
2. *Control and loss:* I want to be separate from these parents, independent, free. But I don't want to lose them; they're all I've got. Will they hang on to me no matter what I do?
3. *Sexuality:* These feelings—I exist because a man and a woman had feelings like these. If I make a baby, will I feel attached to someone? Will this emptiness go away?

These are big issues for most teens, and bigger for adopted teens. We will examine each area below.

The Identity Puzzle

Identity: inner sameness and continuity of one's meaning for others. This textbook definition is a struggle for any teen to achieve. Like a puzzle with assorted pieces that must be examined, turned, and placed together, kids take the pieces of family, interests, appearance, and abilities—genetic and environmental pieces—and see how they fit.

Adopted teens have a complicated puzzle. Some genetic pieces are missing. They may not like some pieces. Remember watching your child position a puzzle piece the wrong way and then pound it with his or her little fist to *make* it go into place? Adopted teens try to make the pieces fit. Integrating the pieces of their lives is frustrating. And you, as their parent, feel their frustration and anger. At times you are a bystander and can only watch. At other times, the anger and frustration are directed at you. Sometimes you can help. Sometimes you cannot.

At some time, most adopted kids think, "Why did they give me away? What was wrong with me?" Explanations can include finances and life circumstances. But most teens need large doses of reassurance that they were not given up or rejected because they were unacceptable or inadequate. Parents who have told their child that he or she was "chosen" may see that special label backfire. The teen feels he must be "extra-able" or exceptional to live up to fantasized expectations. In fact, the expectations may not be fantasy.

Parents who adopt are often financially secure and have adequate time for career development. Following in their footsteps may be more difficult than it is for kids in other families. It is not unusual for professional parents with high energy and goals to experience a poor fit with laid-back, artistic kids who they just cannot understand. Incorporate the higher incidence of adopted kids with ADD and Fetal Alcohol Syndrome (which these parents may not even know exists in their child, although they see different behavior), and good fit is almost impossible. Adopted kids have increased potential for feeling out of touch with their parents.

This all-important developmental task of forming an effective identity takes on a new dimension as maturing young adults try to discover who they are, what they can do well, their strengths and weaknesses. This inner sameness and continuity of one's meaning for others is elusive. Adopted teens ask themselves which connection will help them complete their puzzle, the social bond or biological bond? It is not surprising that teens begin to search for more information about their birth parents.

Satisfactory answers for our sons at age seven were inadequate at age ten. At age seventeen, all details were up for scrutiny. John looked at two tall and narrow parents who love racquetball and running and who never left a homework sheet unfinished through thirty-eight years of combined education. (Well, maybe a few!) He gained weight looking at a piece of pizza, hated to sweat, and would much rather listen to music than do homework. "I weigh 210 pounds. I bet my first dad was fat and hated homework!" he said laughingly after a visit to the scales. Researchers call this "integrating his two genealogies."

Four ways of coping with identity crisis:

1. *Identity achievement.* The individual consciously experiences crisis and tries to resolve it by exploring alternative roles. After trying on different values, he or she makes a commitment to a particular identity and set of values (usually after adolescence).

2. *Moratorium.* The individual confronts questions but does not achieve resolution or commit to a particular path. Being in moratorium is not a long-term solution. It is destabilizing and uncomfortable. Eventually the person moves to identity diffusion or achievement.

3. *Identity foreclosure.* This looks good, but the individual committed to an identity prematurely, before he or she had a chance to experiment with alternatives. No crisis is ever recognized or confronted.

4. *Identity diffusion.* The individual avoids confronting an identity crisis or seeking out alternatives and is unable to make a commitment to a particular identity such as career, sexual orientation, or a set of moral values. This may happen because a child lacks either a support system that would allow him or her to ask troubling questions or a parent figure sufficiently appealing to identify with. The child moves through adolescence unsure of what he or she wants, unwilling to confront the options, and unable to identify with a nurturing figure because none is available.*

*David M. Brodzinsky, Marshall D. Schechter, and Robin Marantz Hening, *Being Adopted: The Lifelong Search for Self* (New York: Doubleday, 1992).

A common coping technique that adopted teens try in their attempt to integrate social and biological bonds is instant maturity. Adopted teens in crisis run away more frequently, move out, act out, or jump into something "adult." Most discover that their rapid separations from their adoptive families result only in greater feelings of emptiness.

Most return. And most determine that the social bond is more satisfying than the biological bond. May I reassure you adoptive parents whose kids are searching. You fear that the other mom and dad will replace you. Research shows that adoptive kids, by an overwhelming majority, end up calling their adoptive parents Mom and Dad. Comforting, isn't it?

Control and Loss

If you are parenting an adopted teen who is not in stormy circumstances, give thanks. If your son or daughter can get through this period without hurting himself or herself and his or her future due to poor judgment calls, you are fortunate.

If you are parenting an adopted teen in crisis, understand that you cannot fill the void in him caused by the reality of adoption. You cannot compensate for his loss or become the missing puzzle piece.

At some time, most adopted children feel abandoned. They grieve a host of losses at different ages. I remember my adopted cousin arguing vehemently with his father, my uncle. I later learned that Peter (my cousin) was forbidden to use his mother tongue (German) for a period of time. This is understandable as my uncle was a soldier during World War II. That house rule got to Pete big time. His first language was *him* and he didn't want it squelched. Adoptive parents may at one time see their teen's denial of the adoption factor, at another time their anger. During the teen years, anger may dominate. All teens must accomplish the developmental task of assuming control of their lives. Because adopted kids' identities may be more fragile, taking control of their lives is more frightening.

Whether you are ready or willing to relinquish control in your teen's life may be irrelevant. His or her leave-taking may make it a given. Trust what training you have already given to your child/adult. It may help you to make these two lists. List one: What positive controls can I offer my teen? List two: What can I no longer control (positives and negatives)? We'll return to this topic at the end of the chapter.

Teens may use the adoption issue as leverage when they are struggling for freedom and emancipation. "I don't like it here—these rules, these people. I've got somebody else out there. My *real* parents will let me be me." They may threaten to run away or actually leave. The fourth time our son ran away, he called home after two days to explain. "I've got to find out if what I'm doing is for you, or me."

Adoptive parents may be tempted to let their adopted teen cross their own boundaries. They see the young person making poor choices, running away, and a host of other acting-out stuff with negative consequences. Hanging tough is incredibly difficult. But your survival and theirs depends on it. In reality, remaining the secure family they've grown up in, with your special personality, traditions, and warts, is what they will eventually come back to. Your family will be different with more tolerance for variation and a greater capacity to accept differences. Nevertheless, that's your family.

Searching for more information about birth parents and siblings may be part of your teen's fantasy in running away. One became a crowd watcher, convinced she might see someone who looked like her somewhere. Many ask more questions and ask if you'll help or interfere with their search. Most teens, when given a choice about finding their birth parents, choose not to. It's having the choice that is important to them.

Sexuality

Sex is a loaded issue for most teenagers. For the adopted teen there is likely to be additional heavy stuff. They are informed enough to recognize that, in many cases, they are adopted because their biological mother and father were not sexually responsible. This realization becomes clear during a stage when they are deciding whether to take identity from their social bond or biological bond.

Pamela became pregnant at age fifteen, the age her birth mother had delivered her. She became pregnant intentionally, to do for her baby what her birth mother could not do. "No way will I give my baby up." However, two years later when other things crowded out her original desire, she relinquished her daughter. Adoptive parents often look on in fear, wondering what adolescent hormones will do to their precious child. There is no easy bandage. Given that running away is more frequent, street conditions are what we described earlier, and teens' worlds are as they are, adoptive parents' concerns are justified.

Our challenge is to resist overreacting. Open discussion, giving what information we have, comforting when we can, without enabling, are gifts that we can give to our teens. We cannot take responsibility for all their behavior in any area, including their sexuality.

Janet's adopted daughter gave birth to a son when she was sixteen. Janet evolved from grandmother to mother because her daughter simply did not take care of her baby. Through months that stretched into years, Janet worked, cared for her ill husband, and acted as mother to her grandson. After an open adoption through which Janet grieved like a mother rather than a grandmother, Janet explained to her daughter, "I'll never do that again. Your next child is *your* child and my grandchild."

Adoptive parents cannot determine their teens' sexual behavior, but they can set their own boundaries on the type of support they will offer in different situations. They can support by communicating, encouraging, and holding their teen accountable.

Giving freedom to search often helps reduce acting-out behavior, including sexual promiscuity. A little information often provides more satisfaction than parents expect.

What Helps

I have a message for adoptive parents from a host of mothers and fathers like you. *Build on your child's strengths.* Having talked to adoptive parents, including ones who are now great-grandparents, this was the universal message they wanted to convey to their counterparts. One couple, now in their seventies, with thirteen children, both biological and adopted, said, "It's important for all teens, but it's essential for your adopted ones. Strengthen the skills they want to develop. Support their ideas. It's as vital as the air they breathe."

Look for something that you can help your child develop. The goal is not to develop a professional artist or athlete, but rather to help your teen feel that "I can" feeling.

My husband felt that our younger son's affectionate nature was a strength. So he has allowed him a procession of dogs to train and nurture. I prefer a "no pet" family. I smelled enough animals growing up on a farm to last a lifetime. I reluctantly admit, however, that Robb is thriving and does quite well at dog training. Why my husband's patience persists is puzzling, considering what he stepped in last night making his way barefooted across the utility-room floor in the dark. With a sick puppy and rugs that needed washing . . . I'll spare you the details.

Yes, it does take energy, patience, and God's greatest dose of grace. However, adoptive parents who've made it farther than we have say it's worth it.

The chorus of adoptive moms and dads had another message: clearly communicate your boundaries to your teen. They all quickly added that agreeing on boundaries was not always easy. Parents can get away with some disagreement—*unless your kids are adopted and/or going through crisis.* Then if parents don't stand together, it's unlikely they'll stand at all.

Get all the help you can. Adoptive parents, because of their maturity and stability usually do—and that's good. Our son understands himself better than many teens do. Therapy and counseling have led him to that place. Could we have made it together without it? I don't know.

Since adolescents are not noted for talking to their parents at some times and on some topics, this tool might help. Ask your teen to complete the sentences. (You might do it for fun at the same time.)

Who Am I?

Read the sentence and complete it with the first thing that comes to your mind as a way to finish the sentence. Then do the same for all twenty sentences. You can write anything that tells you who you think you are—something you do, something you feel, or anything. Work quickly!

1. I am someone who_____ .
2. I am someone who_____ .
3. I am someone who_____ .
4. I am someone who_____ .
5. I am someone who_____ .
6. I am someone who_____ .
7. I am someone who_____ .
8. I am someone who_____ .
9. I am someone who_____ .
10. I am someone who_____ .
11. I am someone who_____ .
12. I am someone who_____ .
13. I am someone who_____ .
14. I am someone who_____ .
15. I am someone who_____ .
16. I am someone who_____ .
17. I am someone who_____ .
18. I am someone who_____ .
19. I am someone who_____ .
20. I am someone who_____ .

Lean on your church, friends, and relatives. Get professional help, both medical and psychological. No one source will be the magic wand. But a team effort will help you through.

When my children were small, I taught Bible studies regarding the gift of children. I stood before hundreds of women and affirmed that all life is given by God. Our children are ultimately his, whether born to us or adopted. We hold them with an open hand, I said, like a bird. God's children are not to be clutched tightly.

During one lonely night when my son was gone, I saw a mental image of him as that bird who had decided to take flight. I had mouthed the words; now I was required to live the message. "Yes, God, he was yours all along, not mine. I will trust you to look out for him, not because you told me to, I feel like it, and my faith is strong, but because I have no other choice."

Faith grows in strange valleys. From our dreams of adoption beside that Wisconsin lake to the realities of parenting, we have discovered so much of what we cannot do. We are living the message: *When we cannot, God can.*

⌐ 13 ⌐

How to Parent the Teenager Inside You

Lauren had immense, trusting blue eyes. Her natural white-blond hair, charm, and infectious smile won teachers on the first day of the semester. She came prepared to class, did her homework, and entered into class discussion. She volunteered for extra projects, asked appropriate questions, and was always "on task." In the middle of her junior year, an *F* appeared on her semester report card in United States History.

"Lauren. This isn't like you. What's going on?"

"I can't keep up with everything. It's no big problem. I'll make it up in summer school." She always sounded believable.

Mid-quarter progress reports were worse. When I

saw her occasionally in the halls, she looked tired. Her usual carefully-put-together look was changing. I stopped in her homeroom one morning. She had gone to sleep, tousled head on her desk. I touched her lightly.

"Lauren, do you have a minute? Let's talk in my office." She followed, waking up as we made our way through the crowded hallways. In my office I did something I seldom do with students.

"Would you like a cup of coffee?" I asked, as I nudged the door shut, closing out the din of the outer office. She looked relieved. What had seemed like no big problem a few weeks ago had mushroomed. Lauren was struggling.

Her two teenage brothers were getting in trouble. One had been hospitalized after taking "bad" drugs. The other was refusing to go to school. Her dad's short fuse regularly ignited. He could no longer push his boys around; they literally fought.

"I'll rip that earring out of your ear!" he had shouted at one son.

You can clutch the past so tightly to your chest that it leaves your arms too full to embrace the present.

"Go ahead and reach for it" had been the taunt. When the fight started, Lauren and her mom left the house. The higher the conflict level at home, the closer Lauren and her mom became. Lauren began to take on more responsibility, trying to prevent circumstances that might cause an argument. Mom was increasingly immobilized by her confusing, frightening circumstances.

As Lauren sat hugging her knee and cradling her

coffee with both hands, I saw a girl/woman who was actually doing quite spectacularly at school, considering what was going on at home.

"Mrs. Neff, wanna see my English assignment?"

"I sure do. What unit are you on?"

"Poetry. My favorite." She dug into an oversized satchel and extracted a neat notebook. She carefully laid the following on my desk.

Mother Child

Two
Cups of coffee,
One broken heart.

She lays her
Tired tears and
Deserted dreams
At the foot of my bed.

And as night hours
Slip into the day,
The soul of a child,
Injured and forgotten,
Cries out for reassurance.

I search to the very ends of my
Limited wisdom
For a way to make it
"All better"
As she has done

For me
Countless times
Before.

And so our talk
Echoes in the darkness.
Mother to mother,
Child to child.

—Lauren Mitchell

Was this Lauren, the irresponsible student who was behind in History? Hardly. This was Lauren, the responsible adolescent whose priorities had shifted as she tried to hold her family together.

Family has accurately been described as a delicate mobile with each piece affected by the slightest movement of another. Many families survive the infant, school-age-child years with a few gentle breezes. Children becoming teens seems to call in a strong wind.

We looked at one reason for this in chapters 2 and 4: the world is different, so families have a unique and increasingly difficult role helping a young person enter adulthood.

A second reason that strong winds increase at this stage is that parents have to face their own issues in a new way when their child becomes a young adult. Parents see their dreams for their children either coming true, fading, or being destroyed before their eyes. Parents see their teens making their own decisions about sexuality, about becoming independent, about intimacy.

The teenager inside us seems to reawaken and want to live in our offspring.

The caring parent in us wants our teen to have it all. We want them to avoid the mistakes we made. These are normal wishes. Many of us run into trouble defining what "it all" is. What is it that we want for our teens? I catch myself wanting for my kids what I wanted at their age and couldn't have.

Or I catch myself wanting something for my children, because their having it or achieving it meets a need in *me,* not them. Our teenagers look directly into our eyes or down on us. We see bits and pieces of our own personality blossoming in their young-adultness. We relate in a new way to their feelings. And this can be good. It's okay to empathize.

I watched my sons drive around the corner in our convertible. The top was down for the first spring-cool evening; they seemed to have no cares in the world. I felt their freedom as if thirty years had dropped off my life.

Genie Lee was picking me up in his pink convertible. This poor farm girl was not riding the bus to school today! I had been offered a *ride.* I can still remember the southern Indiana spring air, the scent of fresh-plowed earth mingled with sweet-blooming locusts. The redbud and dogwood were more beautiful than ever when viewed from a convertible. What pleasure. What freedom.

There's nothing wrong with enjoying our teens' pleasures. But needing those pleasures for our own fulfillment places a great burden on them. Needing success to fulfill two people's lives is simply too much pressure on any one person. Teens may feel as though they are living life for themselves *and* their parents.

One young mother carried such sadness that I feared for her ability to go on. Her daughter was pregnant and wanted to keep her baby. Though continuing school was an option, Laurie was choosing not to. After Laurie left my office to clean out her locker, her mom's tears flowed. She had to sit in silence for a while before she could speak.

"Seventeen years ago, that was me." Her fears finally spilled out. "I wanted more for her. Look at my job. . . . It's so hard."

We had no instant easy answers that day, but mother and daughter left with information on how to get the Graduate Equivalent Degree. I encouraged Mom to get her diploma for *herself.* She promised me she'd look into our community college's evening classes.

"I guess Laurie's not gonna make up for what happened to me." Her voice sounded resigned, but there was a bit of hope creeping in. "I gotta do this for me."

Write your wish list for your teen. Then write beside each wish why that wish is important to *you.* Most parents find they know themselves better after this exercise. One more step is necessary if this list is to be helpful for your teen—and for you! Write across the whole list: "I cannot give these to my teen. I cannot live these for my teen."

It is less painful to freely give up your expectations than have them taken away.

Many adults profit from taking their wish list for their teen on the privacy of a long walk or to some quiet corner of their world, remembering their own teen experiences. Asking, "Why is that on my wish list?" may be an important step in either letting your teen grow up, or releasing your own pain.

Usually if we feel strongly—and I mean an unexplainable, driving desire—that our teen *must* have or *must* achieve something, one of the following motivators lies within us. We parents commonly uncover:

- recognition we hungered for
- opportunity beyond our reach
- intimacy we never experienced

It is difficult work to separate good, healthy, valid wishes for recognition, opportunity, and intimacy from a driving desire that pushes our teens to live for us. Just to recognize these facts from our adolescent teen years can bring change and freedom to our relationships with our teenagers. We may be able to talk about some personal wishes with our young almost-adult, but some may need to be kept inside or shared with another adult, not our child.

I commonly see fathers who want athletic achievement for their sons. Sometimes it's for the applause of the community or coworkers. At times it's a quiet inner thing of recognition that Dad couldn't get. Perhaps an opportunity he couldn't take because of poverty, shyness, or any number of reasons drives Dad's desire.

I observed a mother place her daughter in situations of unwise sexual risk. Mom's teen circumstances prevented her from healthy friendships with young men. Her weight and appearance continued to be a barrier in social relationships (perhaps intentionally). I know that by the time I met this mother, her vicarious living through her daughter was unhealthy for this adult woman and devastating to her daughter.

Whether our wish list seems large or insignificant, giving up our expectations is an important step.

As Christian parents, we can take comfort that God knows our young person better than we do. Our child's Creator knows her strengths and what she can achieve. He knows her weaknesses and personality characteristics. We also know that God can take rough life experiences and use them for his glory—though none of us desire those rough experiences for our child.

It's okay to grieve our losses. It's okay to cry out to God and say, "It's not what I wanted! It's not what I expected! It's not fair!" Our caring God never holds our honesty with him against us. The God I have come to know in Scripture can handle my anger. My lost expectations and broken dreams are not too heavy to dump on him.

Grief has its reasons and stages. Let yourself experience it. It is freeing to grieve, admit our feelings, and put our losses into some kind of livable perspective. I believe that it's imperative for parents to go on and for their teens to move beyond crisis.

It is not uncommon for a mom or dad who think they are in love with another man or another woman to find they are in love with a missing piece of their teenage years. How much healthier to grieve the loss and create a livable way to go on, rather than to keep searching for the missing piece.

Parents who lacked intimacy in childhood or adolescent years can release that loss and look for appropriate ways to build intimacy in adult relationships rather than expect their teens to fill the void.

The easiest parent path is to pass on to our teens the voids, addictions, or problems we experienced. Seeing teens in pain or crisis often brings parents to the realization and commitment that, though difficult, they will do the grief work to leave their broken pieces from childhood and adolescence and not pass them on to their kids.

We see in ourselves the losses of having a critical parent, an absentee parent, an addictive parent, an abusive parent, a chronically ill parent, or one who is rigid and dogmatic or over-indulgent. We can ask ourselves, *How can I become whole from my loss?* rather than *How can my teen make up for my loss?*

Broken Dreams

As children bring their broken toys with tears
    for us to mend,
I brought my broken dreams to God because he
    was my friend
But then instead of leaving him in peace to work
    alone,
I hung around and tried to help in ways that
    were my own
At last I snatched them back and cried
"How can you be so slow?"
"My child," he said, "What could I do?
You never would let go."

—*Author Unknown*

When our broken dream is our personal satisfaction lived through our teen, we hang on tenaciously—until we see our true motive. Then our love for our child compels us to let go.

Moving On

Something beautiful happens in parents who recognize the teen inside them and release their teen from living for them. These moms and dads experience a new beginning. Fortunately, the stage coincides with their child no longer needing to be bathed, fed, and held tightly in the shopping center. Parents have time and physical energy to follow some dreams of their own for themselves.

Teens still require great emotional investment, and crisis is draining. But we do move on. I have watched mothers go back to night school and actually be thrilled to memorize accounting terms and pore over debits and credits in the wee hours of the morning! I have known middle-aged men who took up tennis (carefully, I might add, lest they strain their backs). These moms and dads had been immobilized to follow their own dreams until they released their teens.

If you created the wish list above and found it terribly painful to write across that paper, "I cannot give these to my teen. I cannot live these for my teen," I have a suggestion. Before much time passes, begin a new list.

At the top of the page write, "I would enjoy trying . . ." Write at least ten things before you put your pencil down. Let your mind begin to consider what you can pursue in your own life. You have given to your children what you can. Now you can give them freedom to build their lives.

Two picture assignments might help you put your needs in perspective. In *Kids Who Carry Our Pain* (Thomas Nelson Publishers), Dr. Robert Hemfeldt and Dr. Paul Warren suggest drawing a large circle to represent your family. Within the circle draw smaller circles to represent each person, the energy and attention they bring to the family, their importance in family decisions and life-style, their influence and control over others.

Ideally Mom's and Dad's circles should be larger than any child's. However, when the circles are honestly drawn, some find a child (or more than one child) has larger circles than the parents.

Another picture assignment is to draw a large box representing family. Outside the box draw smaller boxes representing each person. In the family box, write the family activities and what is important in your family life.

Ask each member to write in their outer box what is important in their personal life. For example, if Carrie's family (from chapter 1) had completed this assignment, the family box would have been nearly empty, and Dad's box even more blank. If either parent's box is near empty, new balance is needed.

Look at the two pictures you've drawn. If your circle is tiny and your box empty, become a good parent to yourself. Instead of writing ten things you would enjoy trying, write fifteen. Give yourself permission to take care of yourself. Consider what you can do with your wishes for recognition, opportunity, and intimacy.

Remember, God gave you strengths and weaknesses,

gifts and abilities, just as he did your teen. Parenting may be one reality in your life, but not your sole reason for existence. As you give your teen permission to live his or her own teen years, give yourself permission to move on.

← 14 →
And They Lived Hopefully Ever After

To promise "happily ever after" would be fantasy. But to live with hope is a *real* possibility for any family, regardless of the crises faced. Families whose teens have faced crisis stare at a different "ever after" than other families. Each individual in the family changes. And it can be good.

Perhaps the greatest gift you can give your adolescent after crisis is being a growing, content, and reasonably together person, at the same time you are a parent. Maybe a paraphrase of Luke 10:27 would illustrate. Jesus said, "You must love your neighbor just as much as you love yourself." May I paraphrase that? "You must love your adolescent just as much as you love yourself."

Hold yourself in the same regard that God does and treat yourself accordingly. This is healthy self-love. Then love your teenager in the same way. Hold her in the same regard as God does. Treat her accordingly.

> **Everything can be taken from a parent but one thing: the freedom to choose his/her attitude in any given set of circumstances.**

This is a different theology of parenting than is popular today. This theology mirrors the example from Deuteronomy in which children grow up, not as the primary focus of the adults in their lives, but as people in process, walking alongside parents in process, learning by observation, learning from in-the-trench living, learning by osmosis.

The indirect message of Deuteronomy is quite important: While you parent, go on being a person.

We have lost this perspective because the world's view of life has crowded out God's original idea. Here are a few contrasts:

World's View	God's View
• Since there is no God, parents are the givers of life.	• God is the giver of life.
• Teens are extensions of parents; therefore, teens must succeed for parents to have succeeded.	• Teens are God's creations.
• Since there is no God, I must solve all problems.	• Sin exists in the world; I am an accountable parent, but I am not all-powerful.
• The promise of a better future for my child is my reward for parenting.	• The future is unknown, but it is in God's hands.

While all Christian parents struggle not to be sucked into living by the world's view, parents of teens in crisis have a real battle. When we are looking for solutions so desperately, it is easy to get out of touch with our convictions and get off balance.

One voice whispers, "Be uninvolved. You've failed. Avoid that for which you are unprepared. Focus on work, getting ahead, committee meetings, a good cause, or your favorite hobby. Avoid your teen's crisis. Maybe it or he will go away."

Or a different voice whispers, "Be *involved.* Your teen needs your emotional energy, your time, your life savings. His issues and problems are your issues and problems. Let the appearance of your living space go to pot, your health and your appearance, too. Your teen is troubled, you know."

Middle Ground: How to Find It

Middle ground is hard to find and equally difficult to maintain. Consider that what is good for you may be good for your adolescent. The following items are "good for both."

Be Real

An imperfect parent with integrity is better than fake goodness. Real people apologize for their mistakes. Real people admit that they don't have all the answers. Real people keep commitments to the extent they can. Parents are people. Real people work, rest, and play. Real people are growing spiritually, not spiritual giants.

Communicate

"They don't listen to me! They don't even know me!"

I hear either of these complaints or both frequently as I listen to what teens say about their parents.

Adolescents feel they are being heard when their parents attempt to get in touch with their feelings. Teens do not so much expect parents to answer all their questions or have solutions for their problems. They want to know that parents are willing to listen to them, even if they don't understand. Listening goes a long way.

```
                    Teen Turnoffs
    judging                being too busy
    lecturing              not giving explanations
    criticizing            reacting with anger
    not listening          using sarcasm
    nagging
```

When parents listen, they are more likely to know their teenagers. (Notice my ambiguous "more likely.")

I took an informal poll of several teens and asked them this question: "What bugs you the most in trying to communicate with your parents?" Four things topped the list: being nagged at, being talked down to, being overreacted to, and not being taken seriously.

Now, I realize that "overreacting" is in the eye of the beholder. Our son recently asked quietly, "Can I borrow some money?"

"How much?" we quietly responded.

"Two hundred forty dollars," he quietly replied.

"WHAT!" we chorused loudly in unison.

To our teen this was an overreaction. To parents who possessed nickels and dimes when we were teens, this was an appropriate reaction.

Kids have told me of parents who respond to everything with rage. Often when I call their homes, the background noise level confirms their report. A request for someone to come to the phone becomes an argument with expletives. Small issues escalate in the time that a cat winks. These teens have a hard time learning how to negotiate.

Kids tell me that they are able to ignore parents who nag. From their comments, nagging is merely wasted vocal practice by parents. Teens don't respond more readily or listen better because of repetition.

I can't document this but it seemed that the teens who thought they were talked down to were the younger kids in families. Maybe birth order is a factor. However, all teens wanted to be heard as if they are persons, persons with questions, feelings, and opinions.

Christian parents have an advantage in learning to listen because we have a role model. God always hears us whether we speak, cry, call, or yell. He listens whether what we are saying is wise or foolish, thoughtful or impulsive. He responds to us from where we are rather than where others think we should be, or he knows we could be. He listens. He listens when we ask him to help us listen.

How to Listen When You Don't Like What You're Hearing

1. *Be cool.*
   Take a deep breath and focus on what your teen is saying rather than the response on the tip of your tongue. "You think_____; I think_____. We seem to disagree. Let's talk about it."

2. *Be askable.*
   Teens sense your openness to talk about a subject. If you are closed on an idea, they won't ask about it. And they need more information badly; they may need your input.

3. *Be interested.*
   Teens know your body language. Show them you believe that what they have to say is important.

4. *Listen to their words.*
   Ask questions to clarify a point you may misunderstand. Your active listening increases their self-respect.

5. *Listen to their feelings.*
   Feelings are neither good nor bad, so don't argue with your kids when they tell you how they feel. If you belittle their feelings or discount them, they interpret that you are saying, "I don't care about you."

6. *Clarify what you expect.*
   Teens can't read minds. They, too, have a hard time hearing what they don't want to hear or disagree with.

7. *Judge the action, not the person.*
   "I'm upset that you did not keep your word and call to tell me you were at Matt's house"; not "Won't you ever grow up and act like a responsible human being?"

8. *Listen to your tone of voice.*
   How would you respond to someone speaking to you in the tone of voice that you are using?

Many of us close down to demands from other adults. Teens are people, too.

9. *Remember your adolescence.*
   Don't preach about it, or relive it. But remember how you wanted to be respected. Remember how difficult it was to communicate your thoughts and feelings to your parents.

10. *Call your teen's bluff.*
    They don't really mean everything they say. Giving in to their every demand is giving them opportunities they cannot handle or power to make unwise choices. An appropriate response to "I'm quitting school!" may be "That's not one of your options while you are living at home" (stated calmly, of course).

Discover Feeling Fingerprints

In order to respect your own feelings or the feelings of others, you must be aware of them. One thing we learned through our teen's crisis is that as a family we were unaware of some members' feelings. In order to respect feelings, you have to know them—know feelings in you and feelings in your teen.

This is a new adventure for some parents, especially if in your family of origin you didn't talk much about what was going on inside. In my growing-up family, I don't recall ever being asked, "How do you feel about that?"

Look for signs of different feelings. Discover your own "feeling fingerprints." Look for signs of different feelings in others. Some people can ask themselves, "What am I feeling?" and answer accurately. Not all of us.

What signs tell you that something is bothering you? Some are Stomach People. Indigestion speaks, "Hello! There are strong feelings in here." Others are Sweaty-Palm

People. Then there are the Neck People. "How are you feeling?" you ask them. They turn their head stiffly with a cracking sound. "Fine," they reply. (Yeah, right.)

There are Stiff-Shoulder People and Headache People. Then there are the Flushed-Face People. Women dominate in this category. These are feeling fingerprints. For those of you in touch with your feelings, you know what you are feeling and probably why. If you are *not* one of those parents, you might ask yourself the following questions: I feel my fingerprint; my face is hot or my stomach upset. Why? Am I feeling angry? sad? nervous? tense? What is the problem? What do I want to have happen? Why is this important to me? Put each message in an "I" sentence, taking responsibility for your own feelings.

Change: With a Servant Attitude

Becoming a teenager means separating oneself from family of origin. This necessitates having some information that is yours only, space that is yours only, and sometimes values that are yours only.

**How to Give Effective
Instruction and Guidance**
- Describe rather than judge.
- Be specific rather than global or general.
- Be current (immediate) rather than past-oriented.
- Be task-involved rather than ego-involved.
- Describe behavior rather than the person.

In fact, being family for an adolescent is an artistic balance between being flexible enough to accommodate their differences and being unmovable granite that remains stable while they push away with all their might. Because teens are not fully independent, we find ourselves needing to give direction without threatening and demanding.

Knowing your teen while letting go is a delicate waltz. While adolescents must move away, they desire the security of attachment. While they explore their differences, they may return for assurance to the familiar. During this delicate waltz, our attitude as parents is crucial. A slave attitude creates either an adolescent tyrant or a parent tyrant. A servant attitude looks out for the teen's welfare in unselfishness, to achieve God's goals in the child becoming an adult.

The following attitudes help teens separate successfully from family.

1. "I am committed to setting clear boundaries and expectations." (Even returning young adults need to know courteous guidelines for living with parents.)

2. "I will try to understand your feelings as you leave this house." (This is tough when you want to focus on your own feelings, which may be strong.)

3. "I will allow you to fail. I will walk with you if you will allow me. But I cannot walk for you."

4. "I will encourage relationships with peers and adults outside the family."

5. "I am committed to helping you learn that the secret of life is coping, not mastering."

6. "I will do what I perceive is in your best interest to help you walk out the front door successfully."

One action that parents can take as teens get older and prepare to leave home is *strategic rules reduction.* In corporations, this means cutting out unnecessary guidelines. In organizations, it means eliminating what inhibits creativity. In families, it means stopping squabbling over what's unimportant.

Because families are increasingly diversified, there is no "squabble list" that applies to all families. However, families do well to discuss their own family "un-necessities." In my office, kids tell me about battles their parents are still fighting with them, even though the parents have lost—they just don't know it. Most parents would admit that rules about eating habits and clothes colors are "un-necessities." Most rules vary by family. Freedoms may vary depending on whether there are younger children in the family who are still in process.

If there is a question, apply these guidelines: Can I control that if my teen does not wish to comply? If I insist on this rule, what do I gain and what do I lose? If I insist on this rule, what does my teen gain and what does she lose? Wiser, older parents than I have said, "Choose your battles."

Review our paraphrase from Jesus as your family sorts out the unnecessities. Hold yourself in the same regard that God does and treat yourself accordingly. This is healthy self-love. Then love your teenager in the same way. Hold her in the same regard as God does. Treat her accordingly.

Strategic rules reduction will be a relief to your teen; and will simplify your life as well.

Christian parents have a special source of hope that we can lean on. We know that life is not meaningless. We also know that there is more, much more, after this life. Because of these two truths, we can live without answers and with realities that don't make sense and are not fair—because this life is not all there is.

I was taxiing my son to a practice. I asked him about a detention slip I had seen on the kitchen table. He was going through an especially difficult time with his attention deficit disorder. At fourteen, his body changes were requiring variations in medication, school was getting more demanding, and he felt the world was on his case—including his mother.

"It's not fair!" He was near tears with frustration and anger.

For some reason, I remembered David complaining to God about the unfairness of wicked people's success. After David vented his questions, he had a sense of being in God's presence and an overwhelming feeling that final judgment cannot be based on what we see today (Psalm 73).

"You're right, son. It isn't fair. I'm sorry you have to struggle. God didn't mean it to be this way. Illness, disease, and ADD wasn't his original idea. You're doing the best you can, and I'm proud of you."

I visualized my son and myself standing before God someday. No more ADD, no more struggle, just two trophies in God's eyes. I was reminded that we are all trophies of God's grace—including adolescents who at times have us pulling our hair out!

We pulled up at the soccer field. He literally exploded out of the car, ready to run off his energy. I silently thanked God for his understanding coach, Victor, who knew how to give him direction.

Competitors say, "It's not over till it's over."

"Over" for parents is not achieved in our lifetime. I

will not know "why" until I am in God's presence. Then God will tell me why, when we adopted, I was paired with a tiny eternal being—with ADD. He will tell my son why he struggled with ADD, why he is in our family. Parents without God cannot lean on this hope, this meaning beyond what we can understand with our human minds.

> **Our best thought-out plan of action, though flawed, is better than inaction.**

If our teens do not acknowledge God, we can take hope in the fact that God can and will reach out to them in ways we cannot imagine. We can take hope in the fact that God loves them more than we do and will not give up due to exhausted energy as we ordinary parents do.

If our teens have acknowledged God, we know that their eternity will be good even though their present looks risky. Part of our personal plan of action is to review why we have hope—daily, if not more frequently.

Peter and John told needy people that they didn't have silver and gold to give, but they'd share what they had. They had a message of hope (Acts 3:1-8). Parents can't give their teens what they don't have. When we have an attitude of hope, we can share it with our teens. It can be unspoken. Hope shines in our actions and attitudes as well as in our words.

"Happily ever after" is for fantasies, not families. "Hopefully ever after" is an achievable reality. It's our choice.

Timely Resources for Today's Parenting Issues

THE NEW DARE TO DISCIPLINE
Dr. James Dobson   0-8423-0507-6
A classic for parents on maintaining order, developing responsibility, and building character.

40 WAYS TO TEACH YOUR CHILD VALUES
Paul Lewis   0-8423-0910-1
Teach kids about life's most important skills and attitudes through these creative, effective ideas.

50 PRACTICAL WAYS TO TAKE OUR KIDS BACK FROM THE WORLD
Michael J. McManus   0-8423-1242-0
Practical examples to help teens deal with the serious issues they face daily.

FAITHFUL PARENTS, FAITHFUL KIDS
Greg Johnson and Mike Yorkey   0-8423-1248-X
Successful Christian parents share methods for instilling values in today's kids.

HOW TO HAVE KIDS WITH CHARACTER (EVEN IF YOUR KIDS ARE CHARACTERS)
Nadine M. Brown   0-8423-1607-8
Identifies specific character qualities and provides related Scripture and activities for developing a child's character.

PARENTING TEENS
Dr. Bruce Narramore and Dr. Vern C. Lewis   0-8423-5012-8
Guide children through the dependent-interdependent struggles of growing up and leaving home.